# Municipal Government and Activities of the City of Milwaukee for 1922 Report of the Common Council of the Activities of the City Departments, Boards and Commissions

Ovid B. Blix

*The Making of Modern Law* collection of legal archives constitutes a genuine revolution in historical legal research because it opens up a wealth of rare and previously inaccessible sources in legal, constitutional, administrative, political, cultural, intellectual, and social history. This unique collection consists of three extensive archives that provide insight into more than 300 years of American and British history. These collections include:

Legal Treatises, 1800-1926: over 20,000 legal treatises provide a comprehensive collection in legal history, business and economics, politics and government.

Trials, 1600-1926: nearly 10,000 titles reveal the drama of famous, infamous, and obscure courtroom cases in America and the British Empire across three centuries.

Primary Sources, 1620-1926: includes reports, statutes and regulations in American history, including early state codes, municipal ordinances, constitutional conventions and compilations, and law dictionaries.

These archives provide a unique research tool for tracking the development of our modern legal system and how it has affected our culture, government, business – nearly every aspect of our everyday life. For the first time, these high-quality digital scans of original works are available via print-on-demand, making them readily accessible to libraries, students, independent scholars, and readers of all ages.

old books. new life.

**The BiblioLife Network**

This project was made possible in part by the BiblioLife Network (BLN), a project aimed at addressing some of the huge challenges facing book preservationists around the world. The BLN includes libraries, library networks, archives, subject matter experts, online communities and library service providers. We believe every book ever published should be available as a high-quality print reproduction; printed on-demand anywhere in the world. This insures the ongoing accessibility of the content and helps generate sustainable revenue for the libraries and organizations that work to preserve these important materials.

The following book is in the "public domain" and represents an authentic reproduction of the text as printed by the original publisher. While we have attempted to accurately maintain the integrity of the original work, there are sometimes problems with the original work or the micro-film from which the books were digitized. This can result in minor errors in reproduction. Possible imperfections include missing and blurred pages, poor pictures, markings and other reproduction issues beyond our control. Because this work is culturally important, we have made it available as part of our commitment to protecting, preserving, and promoting the world's literature.

**GUIDE TO FOLD-OUTS MAPS and OVERSIZED IMAGES**

The book you are reading was digitized from microfilm captured over the past thirty to forty years. Years after the creation of the original microfilm, the book was converted to digital files and made available in an online database.

In an online database, page images do not need to conform to the size restrictions found in a printed book. When converting these images back into a printed bound book, the page sizes are standardized in ways that maintain the detail of the original. For large images, such as fold-out maps, the original page image is split into two or more pages

Guidelines used to determine how to split the page image follows:

• Some images are split vertically; large images require vertical and horizontal splits.
• For horizontal splits, the content is split left to right.
• For vertical splits, the content is split from top to bottom.
• For both vertical and horizontal splits, the image is processed from top left to bottom right.

# Municipal Government and Activities

OF THE

# CITY OF MILWAUKEE

FOR 1922

# Report of the Common Council

Of the Activities of the City Departments, Boards and Commissions

Compiled and Edited by
OVID B. BLIX,
Municipal Reference Librarian

AUTHORIZED AND PUBLISHED BY THE COMMON COUNCIL

|                                                      | Page |
|------------------------------------------------------|------|
| Classified List of City Officials                    | 4    |
| Statistical Facts about Milwaukee                    | 5    |
| Common Council                                       | 7    |

Executive and Administrative
| Mayor                                              | 11 |
| City attorney                                      | 12 |
| City clerk                                         | 13 |
| Board of election commissioners                    | 13 |
| Board of city service commissioners               | 14 |
| Board of fire and police commissioners            | 15 |
| Criminal courts                                    | 15 |

Public Finance
| Board of estimates                                 | 16 |
| Comptroller                                        | 18 |
| Public debt commissioners                          | 20 |
| Tax commissioner                                   | 21 |
| Central board of purchases                         | 23 |
| City treasurer                                     | 23 |

Public Works and Public Utilities
| Department of public works                         | 24 |
| Sewerage commission                                | 31 |
| Board of harbor commissioners                      | 32 |
| Street railway acquisition committee              | 34 |

Protection of Life and Property
| Police department                                  | 39 |
| Fire department                                    | 39 |
| Fire and police alarm system                       | 40 |
| Building inspector                                 | 40 |
| Board of examiners of stationary engineers        | 42 |
| Bureau of smoke suppression                        | 42 |
| Bureau of weights and measures                     | 42 |
| Safety commission                                  | 42 |

Public Health
| Health department                                  | 43 |
| Johnston Emergency hospital                        | 48 |

City Planning
| Board of public land commissioners                 | 48 |

Public Welfare
| Park board                                         | 51 |
| Garden Homes development                           | 56 |
| Free employment office                             | 56 |

Education
| Board of school directors                          | 57 |
| Local board of industrial education                | 61 |
| Public library                                     | 62 |
| Public museum                                      | 65 |
| Auditorium                                         | 68 |
| Art institute                                      | 69 |

Statistical Appendix
| Building operations                                | 71 |
| Crime                                              | 75 |
| Public finance                                     | 78 |

A. P. Rosenthal, chairman.

...rney, city
John M. Niven.

...dings, inspector of
William D. Harper.

...service commissioners, board of
Otto F. Hoppe, president,
Mark H. Place, chief examiner.

...k, city
John J. Weiher, Jr.

...ptroller, city
Louis M. Kotecki.

...mon council

Cornelius Corcoran, president.
1. Leo Luke Hannifin.
2. Louis Weiss.
3. Cornelius Corcoran.
4. John Koerner.
5. Thomas J. Reynolds.
6. Arthur Shutkin.
7. John Doerfler, Jr.
8. Felix Lassa.
9. Herman O. Kent.
10. Carl P. Dietz.
11. Ole A. Olsen.
12. Joseph F. Drezdzon.
13. Robert J. Landowski.
14. Albert Janicki.
15. Charles W. O'Connor.
16. Arthur Bennett.
17. Paul Gauer.
18. William I. Greene.
19. William Esser.
20. August W. Strehlow.
21. William Baumann.
22. John W. Radke.
23. John L. Bohn.
24. Max J. Elsner.
25. Charles C. Schad.

...commissioners, public
William H. Upmeyer, chairman,
Louis M. Kotecki, secretary.

...tion commissioners, board of
Charles Kaempfer, chairman,
Senator Schultz, secretary.

...ineer, city
Joseph T. Schwada.

...ineers, board of examiners of
Reinhard Kunz, Jr., chief examiner.

...mates, board of
Daniel W. Hoan, president,

Herman Bleyer, secretary.

Health, commissioner of
George C. Ruhland, M. D.

Johnston emergency hospital
R. F. Teschan, M. D., chairman, board of
Minnie P. Getts, superintendent.

Industrial education, board of
James D. Hickey, president,
Robert L. Cooley, director of vocational

Land commissioners, board of public
William H. Schuchardt, president,
Charles B. Whitnall, secretary,
Edward Grieb, real estate agent,
Gardner Rogers, city planning engineer

Library, public
William Kaumheimer, president board of
Matthew S. Dudgeon, librarian.

Mayor
Daniel W. Hoan.

Museum, public
George A. West, president board of
Dr. S. A. Barrett, director.

Park board
Max P. Kufalk, president,
Frank P. Schumacher, secretary.

Police, chief of
Jacob G. Laubenheimer.

Public works, commissioner of
Roland E. Stoelting.

Purchases, central board of
Daniel W. Hoan, president,
Joseph W. Nicholson, purchasing agent

Safety commission
H. E. Bradley, M. D., chairman,
Claude Diegle, secretary.

School board
James H. Derse, president,
Milton C. Potter, superintendent of scho...
Frank Harbach, secretary.

Sewerage commission
George P. Miller, chairman,
T. Chalkley Hatton, chief engineer,
John H. Fowles, secretary.

Smoke inspector
Charles Poethke.

Street railway acquisition committee
Fred S. Hunt, chairman,
Martin C. Glaeser, secretary.

Tax commissioner

ater, square miles_____ .028
y of Milwaukee
otal, square miles_____235

operations
of work done under permit_____$31,287,645
of buildings_____$25,229,580
ts, number issued_____ 40,481
loyes
 number _____ 8,064
 civil service
ity service commission_____ 2,984
ire and police commission_____ 1,448
ing staff _____ 3,026
pt from civil service_____ 606

e, amount of

eceipts, tons _____ 4,355,926
hipments, tons _____ 2,093,472

eceipts, tons _____ 6,476,381
hipments, tons _____ 5,030,742
receipts, tons_____ 3,502,445
 receipts, bushels_____ 62,737,368
 shipments, bushels_____ 48,076,020
y
nt of outstanding bonds_____$28,947,500
limit _____$31,165,500

data
trations, persons _____ 153,804
g precincts _____ 238

City
et 1922 _____$24,006,925
t, 1923 _____$25,464,082

es
nt (estimated) _____ $1,513,000

ic location
ude _____43° 1′ N
itude _____87° 40′ W

Island harbor property
wned by city, acres_____ 41
ow under condemnation, acres___ 43
ew land to be made, acres_____ 76

of first known visit of white man
o Milwaukee _____ 1671
of first permanent white settler_ 1818
permanent white settler__ Solomon Juneau
poration as city_____January 31, 1846

ownership
er _____ 106,101
d by occupant _____ 37,386
from incumbrance_____ 14,994
gage debt on homes, estimated____$58,000,000
t
(estimated) _____ 8

public
lation by system_____ 2,479,332
nes in system_____ 495,547
wers _____ 106,224
s of distribution, total_____ 1,186
(manufacturing, jobbing, wholesale)
s _____ 1,600

Number _____
Area, acres _____
Center plots in boulevards, lineal feet_  34
County system
Number _____
Area, acres _____

## Population

U. S. Census, 1920_____ 457
Census bureau estimate, July 1, 1923_  484
Foreign born in city_____ 110
Milwaukee county _____ 539
Wisconsin _____ 2,632

## Refuse, municipal collection and disposal

Ash and refuse collection, cubic yards_  465
Garbage collect... tons_____ 47
Mixed refuse incinerated, tons_____ 55

## Schools
Public
Graded _____
Trade _____
High _____
Social centers _____
Enrollment _____  62
Private and parochial
Catholic _____
Lutheran _____
Others _____
Colleges _____
Continuation _____

## Sewers
Lateral, miles _____
Intercepting, miles _____

## Streets, alleys, highways
City streets
Miles _____
Acreage _____
Pavement
Permanent, miles _____
Macadam, miles _____
Alleys, improved, miles_____
County roads, total miles_____
County roads, concrete, miles_____

## Taxation and assessments
Property subject to taxation, valu-
ation _____$677,07(
Exempt property, valuation_____$ 97,82
Total property valuation_____$856,98
Special assessments _____$ 1,19
Assessments, number _____  19(
Tax rate, city purposes, per $1,000
assessed valuation_____$
Tax rate, city, county, state purposes,
per $1,000 assessed valuation____$

## Vital statistics
Marriages _____ 4,
Births _____ 10,
Birth rate per thousand_____
Births in hospitals_____ 2,
Deaths _____ 4,
Death rate per thousand_____
Average age of death_____
Average ages of death over five_____

*To the People of Milwaukee:*

The Common Council submits this report of the municipal government of your city and the activities of its various departments, bureaus, boards and commissions for 1922. Reports of quasi-public institutions to which the city contributes financial support are also included.

The practice of binding together and issuing departmental reports in a single volume prevailed in this city up to the year 1909. But as these reports were lengthy and the cost of printing high, the practice was discontinued. From that time until 1921 some of the more important departments have been given appropriations for printed reports, but all appropriations for separate reports for departments under the control of the common council were eliminated from the 1921 budget. In lieu thereof provision was made for the publication of a concise, readable, comprehensive report of city work, as an economy measure and as a more adequate method of informing the public of the city's work. The 1921 report included the work of only those departments over which the common council had entire financial control. This report goes a step further and includes reports of the boards and commissions which have independent mill tax levies and of several quasi-public institutions to which the city grants some financial assistance.

The grouping of departments and boards under particular headings is purely abitrary and is followed for the sake of convenience only. Each department and board is independently administered from the other organizations included in the group.

Milwaukee Lake Front

# COMMON COUNCIL

Corcoran, president

aldermen:

eo Luke Hannifin
ouis Weiss
ornelius Corcoran
ohn Koerner
homas M. Reynolds
rthur Shutkin
ohn Doerfler, Jr.
elix Lassa
erman O. Kent
arl P. Dietz
le A. Olson
oseph Drezdzon
obert J. Landowski
lbert Janicki
harles W. O'Connor
aniel L. McWilliams
aul Gauer
Villiam I. Greene
Villiam Esser
ugust. W Strehlow
Villiam Baumann
ohn W. Radke
ohn L. Bohn
Iax J. Elsner
harles C. Schad

J. Weiher, Jr., city clerk
s S. Brand, deputy city clerk
J. Reiff, committee clerk

## municipal authority

rter of the city of Milwaukee provides that
cipal government of the city shall be vested
yor and the common council." This charter
is somewhat restricted by the fact that the
lature, from which the city gets its author-
, has given several boards and commissions
to separate mill taxes largely independent
n council control.

## zation

organization of the common council as the
the popular referendum held in April, 1918
omplete. The hold-over aldermen at large
their terms in April so that the council now
f the twenty-five ward aldermen only. The
in the size of the council brought about a re-
ion of committees and a decrease in their
rom nine to six by a combination and read-
of work.

area from the city of Wauwatosa was declared inv
on the ground that annexation from a city requ
affirmative action from the city council of the
from which it was detached before it could be
nexed to another city. Three ordinances for
annexation of 346.48 acres of territory was a
upon favorably early in 1923. Threatened legal ac
caused the repeal of two of the ordinances covering
annexation of over three hundred acres of land.
petitions are being recirculated and it is expected
the required number of proper signatures will be
cured. Work was also done toward securing si
tures to petitions in the neighborhood west of
city limits to the Soldiers' Home. It is expected
nine hundred acres of territory in this vicinity wi
added to the city.

The task of circulating petitions became so exter
that four extra clerks were allowed to the boar
land commissioners for this purpose.

The anticipated annexation of North Milwaukee
not materialize because, although the residents of
city expressed a desire for annexation in a pop
advisory referendum, they elected a village b
hostile to the movement.

In connection with the campaign for the annexa
of outlying territory the council enacted an ordin
requiring persons living outside the city limits
desired connection with the local water distribu
system, to present annexation petitions or to
contracts giving ninety days notice before water
nections will be made by the city. The latter alte
tive applies generally to persons living in terr
non contiguous to the city limits and was adopte
a method of forcing signature to annexation peti
in the future.

The council is also on record as favorable to
immediate construction of the necessary improven
in the way of streets, water, sewer and street lig
facilities in newly annexed territory. Money i
cluded in the 1923 budget to do this work. W
facilities may be extended to suburbanites just as
as annexation petitions are presented.

## Art institute

The city entered into a contract with the Milw
Art Institute to appropriate twenty thousand do
annually for ten years for the work of that instit
in return for which the institute agreed to turn
to the city, at the end of this period, all its real
erty, buildings, furnishings, equipment, pain

orate in November. Although it was repassed
he 1923 session of the legislature, a popular vote
ot be held until the general election in the fall of
.   As legislative action is necessary after ratifi-
n by the elecorate, there can be no home rule
ter until 1925.

e constitutional amendment providing for an in-
se in the debt limit of municipalities for the pur-
of purchasing revenue producing utilities, which
approved by the council, was defeated by the
orate by a large majority.

## planning

ndemnation proceedings for the widening of
r-Biddle streets were commenced by instructing
ity attorney to draft the proper resolution and
ity engineer to prepare the necessary maps and
ys for the improvement. The width of the street
ixed at one hundred sixty feet from Juneau park
xth street, two hundred sixty feet from Sixth
ghth streets, and three hundred fifty feet from
h to Ninth street.

operty has been purchased in almost every block
the proposed widening to be used as evidence of
values in the condemnation proceedings. The
r of fixing rentals on city owned property at six
ent of the assessed valuation was approved. Man-
ant of this property is vested in the real estate
subject to common council control.

ndemnation of the civic center site of the police
uarters building and the balance of the block
ocupied by the library-museum building adjoin-
he civic center site were ordered. Property in
of these tracts was purchased outright.

committee of aldermen and other city officials
d Kansas City to study zoning, the planning of
bs and methods of park and playground acquisi-
ffective in that city.

rty minor changes were made in the use, height
rea district maps of the zoning ordinance. A
e in the height restrictions in one hundred
y-five foot districts allows one hundred foot
s to be constructed above the height limit, pro-
that the angle formed between the roof line and
aginary line drawn from the outside of the roof
top of the tower is not greater than 63.26 de-
This allows buildings to be erected to the height
feet, provided that the proper set-back is made
ries above the 125 foot level.

## service

general reductions or increases in salaries of city
yes were allowed during the year. However, a
r of positions, where the salaries were inade-
were given special consideration, but the total
ary increases was very small. The elimination
itions by the reorganization of the street illumi-
service and the placing of the Milwaukee River
ig tunnel on a mechanical basis involved a sav-
f thirty-eight thousand dollars. Several new
ns were created to take care of the increasing
of the city. The bridge tenders who now work
day in the year were given one day off in fifteen.

of public indebtedness. As a result the counc
a resolution requesting legislation which wou
the establishment of a public debt amortizatic
be accumulated from

(1) Interest accumulations now in the city

(2) A minimum of one-third of the interes
    lations upon city funds in the future.

(3) All other amounts which the commo
    may from time to time contribute.

Number 1 will furnish approximately two
fifty thousand dollars to start the fund.  N
would have furnished about one hundred fi
sand dollars in 1923.  This fund is to be in a
the funds accumulating to pay principal an
on outstanding and future bond issues of th
Milwaukee bonds and to purchase other muni
government securities.  It will be allowed to
late until the amount of money in the fund
mates three-fourths of the city indebtedn
which three-quarters of the annual interest
will be used to wipe out the principal and th
of the city debt and to finance public impr
which are now financed by the issuance of b

## Fire service

The fire fighting service of the city was inc
the purchase of the fire tug "Torrent" from
company in northern Minnesota.  This tug
larger than any of the fire tugs now operate
fire department and will greatly increase the
of this branch of the service.

## Harbor

The president of the common council at its
appeared before the rivers and harbors com
the House of Representatives to argue in
sanctioning a four million dollar expenditure
construction of a federal breakwater in M
harbor.  The authorizing act was passed by
and signed by the president.  The river and
appropriation bill passed by the last session
gress contained an item of $700,000 to be used
ting the work under way.  Further appropriat
be made by succeeding Congresses to comp
work.  Representatives of the council also
the National Rivers and Harbors Congress a
ington in behalf of the St. Lawrence Watery
ject.

Approval was given to a scale of rates pre
the harbor commission for winter mooring p
in the inner harbor.

## Health

An increase in the efficiency of the health dep
was gained by the reorganization of the denta
and the authorized transfer of the south side
and clinic to larger quarters in a building un
struction.

A location for the nurses' home for the Sou
hospital was secured by the transfer of the
ward yard to the hospital for that purpose.
the money for the erection of the home is to b

system. ... ... ... ... ...
nue and Sixth street, extended across the
be the base lines from which house number-
start. Numbers are to be run one hundred
) the block on all sides of the base line. The
contemplates the elimination of duplicate
es and the substitution of a single name for
t system of separate names for streets on
of the river and valleys crossing the city.

elfth street market was abandoned during
nd its area platted into lots. Shelter sheds
ed on the North
arket. Part of
ard market site
iside for play-
irposes. A new
s established in
/iew section of
n rented prop-

## d playgrounds

gest park ac-
f the year was
acre addition to
park. Several
acquired to
the north east
f Washington
a gift of a com-
rk in the Gar-
s area was ac-
Several other
triangles and
were obtained.
or the purchase
ns to Lincoln
ioldt parks and
ition of a large
l in the six-
d were refused.
of public land
ners was in-
o make a sur-
playground and
spot needs of
d to devise ways and means of financing park
round acquisitions. An automobile tourist
was established in Lake park.
ration was given to a measure requesting
board to turn over Lapham park and other
playground property under its jurisdiction
k board.

ysical equipment of the police department
ased by provision for the purchase of ad-
otorcycles, the installation of a heating plant
nory so that drill and instruction could be
there during the winter months, the con-

Purchase was made of the aerial traffic regulator
use on Third street and Grand avenue. Many ins
lations of mushroom lights were ordered at danger
street crossways.

A revision of the ordinance regulating guards
lights about ice cutting fields was made as a p
tective measure.

The safety commission was requested to submit
matters relating to safety and the regulations of p
lic utilities to the council before appealing to the W
consin Railway Commission.

## Public utilities

The common cou
has strenuously oppo
all attempts to introd
the one-man car on
streets of Milwaukee,
the contentions have b
over ruled by the s
railroad commission. I
in the year the city
torney was instructed
start a court action to
termine the validity of
city ordinance requir
street cars to be man
with two employes and
test the right of the r
way commission to m
regulations in this reg

A petition of the st
railway company for
franchise to maintair
trackless trolley on I
coln avenue was der
after it was discove
that the city did not h
authority to grant suc
franchise.

A large program
street railway zone st
repair was approved
the council. This w
is being done and finar
by the local street
way company. The po

City Hall

of allowing the paving of street zones with cement
followed to a large extent.

The council allowed the abandonment of tracks
service upon Chestnut street between Seventh
Twelfth streets with the agreement that there she
be no reduction of service to the district served by
line.

## Public works

Drastic cuts in the 1922 budget made it imposs
to keep up the amount of street construction to
of 1921. Notwithstanding, a great deal of both st
and alley work was ordered.

An investigation of the possibility of crushing s

onstitutional. The decision has been appealed to
United States supreme court.

## hases

e council authorized the making of a number of
rtant contracts, especially of motor equipment
ut requiring formal bidding upon a showing in
instance that this was for the benefit of the city.

en the coal shortage became serious in the fall
count of the closing of mines on account of labor
les earlier in the season and the resulting pooling
al shipments by federal order, the companies hav-
ontracts with the city were allowed rebates for
lity to comply with their contract specifications
the thermal heat units in coal furnished to the

## oads

e council set aside money for the grade separation
ordered by the state railway commission for the
share of the cost of this work as in previous
. The North Western Line began work on the
depression of its Madison division toward the end
e year, and the city engineer had to be allowed
engineering assistance to keep pace with this
As the Milwaukee road is still delaying the com-
ement of work on the plea of lack of funds, the
attorney has been instructed to petition the rail-
commission for an order directing the work to be
at once.

nsideration of the electrification of terminals was
red at the request of the railroads concerned on
round that there was no money available for this
at the present time.

## e disposal

a result of a study of waste disposal by a special
ittee appointed by the president of the common

## Waterworks

The most important decision of the common
in regard to waterworks was to delay the cons
of a water filtration until the results of the o
of the sewage disposal plant, which will be r
1924, upon the city water supply can be det
This decision was due partly to the difficu
financing its construction at this time and p
the fact that the sewerage commission took t
that filtration would be unnecessary when the s
disposal plant was in operation. It further de
use the money raised by the increase of wat
in 1921 for financing the construction of the C
street main, the Riverside pumping station, th
tion and maintenance of the waterworks and su
important purposes as the council might direct

Another important decision of the council
pass a resolution refusing to give connectio
the Milwaukee water works distribution sy
persons living outside of the city limits until t
signed annexation petitions or contracts to a
city to shut off the water, if it sees fit, upon
ing of ninety days notice.

The commissioner of public works was au
to let contracts for the steel work of the sup
ture of the Riverside pumping station.

A transfer of $225,000 from the waterworks
to the general city fund was authorized as in
years.

## Wisconsin League of Municipalities

After an absence of several years the city
the Wisconsin League of Municipalities. This
zation exists to make it possible for municipa
the state to work together efficiently upon ma
common interest for the betterment of munici
ernment and to present a united stand before t
lature in matters affecting their interests.

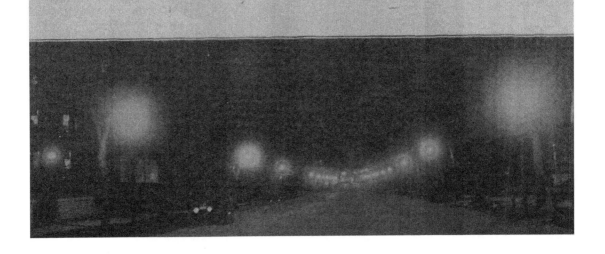

Garden Homes Housing Development

# EXECUTIVE, ADMINISTRATIVE AND JUDICIAL
# MAYOR

. Hoan, mayor
M. Duncan, secretary to the mayor

ayor is the chief executive officer of the city.
it is his duty to see that the state laws and
iances are enforced and that all the officers
y discharge their respective duties. In case
r disturbance he has power to appoint spe-
emen to prevent disorder and preserve the
He appoints the members of the various
ards and commissions and the heads of the
city departments subject, in many cases
to confirmation by a majority of the mem-
he common council.

sident of the board of estimates and the
oard of purchases and a member of the
review, fire and police pension boards and
orium board, he exercises an important part
neral administration of city affairs.

ordinance or resolution passed by the com-
icil is presented to the mayor for approval.
iich he approves he signs and those which
proves, he may veto by returning to the
council with his objections. The common
nay override this veto by a two-thirds vote
embers. Ordinances and resolutions may be-
ective without his signature. He may also
ific items in the budget.

ayor in his official capacity welcomes con-
to the city, entertains official guests, issues
kes licenses and generally studies and looks
general welfare of the city.

e of vacancy or absence the president of the
council exercises all the powers and duties
office is filled or the mayor resumes the
his position.

## banner year

expansion of its industrial and transporta-
lities, 1922 was by far Milwaukee's banner
he building of homes reached the highest
nce 1912. A total of 2,911 families were

The Milwaukee road acquired the Gary line.
belt line service around Chicago avoids the
delay due to freight congestion at that point.
Northwestern road has started the work of aboli
grade crossings on the southwest side. The North
line has installed a first class express servic
Chicago, to the large district south of Chicago
to the Michigan fruit belt.

The street railway company has extended its
ice to Lincoln park and the Wells street car lin
been rerouted over Wells and Oneida streets.
new boat lines have established service to and
Milwaukee. The city has condemned land and st
to build docks upon property needed for our ha
Congress has approved the south breakwater,
assuring Milwaukee of the great outer harbor

The county government has established the
county airport in America. Arterial highways
been developed within and without the city.
have provided motor bus and passenger transp
tion and have made it possible to move freig
truck, all of which has materially relieved our
portation difficulties.

## Labor

During the year leading manufacturers who
located new factories in our city—for example,
ington Patton, E. T. Whelan and Charles W.
have declared that the workers are Milwaukee's
est and best asset. Secretary of Labor Davis
wise has congratulated Milwaukee upon its pea
industrial progress. Let us hope that Wisconsin
whole will recognize the value of its workers by
ing provision for an old age pension system for

## Housing

Our greatest contribution toward paying in
our duty to the workers was in the promotion
Garden Homes project with its one hundred h
The Garden Homes project has advertised Milw
favorably throughout the United States. Stu
everywhere are watching anxiously for the co
tion of this experiment. The construction of
ers' homes in a garden spot with ample playg

ted into modern fire apparatus at a saving of ? per cent of the cost.

he water department has added but two employes ing the last ten years while the service has in-ased forty per cent in volume.

he new commissioner of public works has pro-ssed in the necessary work or reorganizing his artment. Electricity units have replaced gas il-inating units at a saving of eight dollars per unit year with one hundred per cent more light. Three tying bridges have been motorized at an annual ing of $11,500. More modern equipment has re-ed the cost of cleaning and flushing sewers during 2.

Iilwaukee is the only city of its size where ashes removed from the basements by the municipality. other large cities this work must be paid for by home owner, and then, the householder himself st place the ashes in the rear for the private con-:tor. In northwestern cities each family must pay m ten to twelve dollars for this service while in waukee, the city does the same work for four ars. In other cities where garbage is collected private parties the householder pays in the neigh-hood of two dollars per month for this service reas in Milwaukee this work is done by the city a cost of two dollars per year.

## blic indebtedness

Vhile other American cities are allowing their ded indebtedness to increase at an alarming rate, waukee is taking steps which will lead to the mate elimination of her debt. When one remem-s how great a percentage of the city's income is d for debt and interest payments, the importance this movement will be readily recognized. This artment was instrumental in organizing the first c foundation in this country for the accumula- of a fund by contribution and devise by public ited citizens to be used for the elimination of in-tedness. The mayor's secretary was a member of special committee which drew the law for the blishment of an amortization fund out of public ds to assist in the above mentioned purpose.

## ice

he efficiency of the police department has doubled e the shake-up and reorganization of 1921. Mil-ikee is the only large American city that did not erience a severe after-the-war crime wave in e of crime waves elsewhere. While the innum-ble factors contribute to this achievement, the ce department must receive a large share of the lit. A traffic bureau, bureau of identification, an omobile theft squad and a school for police officers police women have all been added during the year. members of the department are receiving instruc- in life-saving and first aid methods. The new ce band, the new pension system, an honest pro-ion system and the alertness of the new officers e all combined to create a fine spirit of co-opera- among the officers and men.

## y growth

he annexation question is now being solved. Dur-

price. The Sebastian Walter and ? gifts to the city have been received.

The inauguration of booster week was o most gratifying events of the year. Such arouses civic consciousness and summarize sults of our progress. It should become affair that all of us may learn more of ea efforts and achievements for the benefit worthy effort in our community.

In conclusion, we should remember that gives greater service to its citizens than large city while its tax rate is among the cities of its size.

## CITY ATTORNEY

John M. Niven, city attorney
Mark A. Kline, first assistant city attorney
Charles W. Babcock, assistant city attorne;
Walter J. Mattison, assistant city attorney
Joseph L. Bednarek, assistant city attorney
Raymond F. Jaekels, assistant city attorney
Leo A. Mullaney, assistant city attorney
Madge E. Mathe, secretary

## General duties

The city of Milwaukee is the largest c in the state of Wisconsin and its activities ably the most varied. An idea of its size m when we consider that the 1922 budget calle expenditure of over twenty-four million do

The city attorney is required to conduct a business of the corporation and of the de thereof, including the independent boards ar er business in which the city shall be intere so ordered by the common council. He m required, furnish written opinions upon sub mitted to him by the mayor, or the common any of its committees, or any other departm municipal government. He must keep a do the cases to which the city may be a par court of record, in which shall be briefly e steps taken in each case. It is also the du city attorney to draft all ordinances, bonds, leases, conveyances, and other such instru writing as may be required by the busine city; to examine and inspect tax and assessr and all proceedings in reference to the le collection of taxes and assessments; and to such other duties as may be prescribed by tl and ordinances of the city.

## Organization

The work of the members of the depa specialized as much as possible, thereby m assistants experts in their respective fields cipal legal work. Thus one assistant handle quisition and condemnation matters, anoth utilities, another finances, another taxation ar questions of charter construction, while sti assistant is detailed to take care of muni district court cases. The secretary of the d handles the details of the workmen's con work.

## paration

separation matters received considerable
of the city attorney's department during
As a result, the Layton park separation
icago and North Western Railway Co., is
ng vigorously pushed. Wider bridges
ered on the arterial highways involved in
seding. A hearing also has been had to re-
Chicago, Milwaukee and St. Paul Railway
ate grades from Center street north to
limits and every effort has been made to
at railroad to begin' its work on the grade
south of Center street.

## te acquisition

usual amount of time was devoted during
eal estate matters. The city acquired more
00,000 of lands for streets, parks, schools,
museum, ward lots, dumping grounds and
rposes, including lands for the widening of
d Biddle streets. Condemnation proceedings
ng for forty-two acres of the Illinois Steel
t south of Jones Island for outer harbor
The city attorney's department has passed
itles and drawn all documents relating to
ls and advised the city officials on all of the
stions relating to the proceedings for the
n of these properties.

matters required a great deal of attention.
erable amount of money was recovered for
on delinquent tax bills, and litigation was
nvolving important questions of assessment
income, personal and real property taxes.
ice was given to taxing officials. An idea of
rtance of this work may be had when we
that there were 80,000 separate real estate
and 45,000 personal property valuations, a
ssment of over $677,000,000.

## 's compensation

ally all of the six thousand or more city em-
under the compensation law and all the de-
lved in the payment of compensation and
t of claims were handled by the city at-
ffice. Whenever an employe is injured while
the fact must be reported at once to the
rney's office. Surgical and hospital treat-
urnished by the city and compensation paid
sability.

## eous matters

ual number of matters involving public util-
ired attention. Among the most important
aring involving gas rates, which resulted in
ard revision of rates. Important litigation
handled involving the relation of Milwaukee
burbs. Among these are the water rates
ich is pending, and the litigation concerning
ation of a portion of the city of Wauwatosa.

handle the clerical end of its work. It is his dut
be present at all its meetings and to keep a full
accurate account of its proceedings. He keeps
official file of all the matters presented to the con
council for consideration. He is custodian of the
seal, and all papers requiring to be sealed wi
must be brought to his office for that purpose.

## Administrative duties

The city clerk is also the head of a depart
which has certain administrative functions.
twenty thousand city orders amounting to twelve
lion dollars were issued from this office during
year. Fifty-six thousand chattel mortgages and
ditional sales contracts were recorded. The net
enue from this source was less than seven thou
dollars which is less than the cost of maintai
the service. Bills to increase the rates for this
were enacted into law by the 1923 legislature.

This department also issues the bulk of the bus
licenses required by the city. These numbered
thousand and brought in a revenue of one hun
and seventy-five thousand dollars. Among the
numerous of these were 2,688 soft drink lice
bringing in a revenue of one hundred and thirty
thousand dollars, 646 of vehicle drivers, 706 of
table establishments with 903 tables, 218 of ex
vehicles, 211 of second hand dealers, 209 of veh
for hire.

## BOARD OF ELECTION COMMISSIONER

Charles Kaemper, chairman
Robert S. Schuffenhauer
William Fenske
Senator Schulz, secretary

## Organization and work

The board of election commissioners is comp
of three members, one from each of the domi
parties as shown by the general election, appo
by the mayor. Before the appointment become
fective, the appointee must be certified as to
bership in the party by the chairman of the
committe of the political party whose represent
he is. The commission conducts all work in cor
tion with elections including the registration of vo
The registry lists are compiled from a card inde
voters kept in the office of the commission. Any
can register at any time during the year by preser
himself or herself at the city hall office. Notice o
moval from one voting precinct to another car
mailed to the office of the board. A special sta
clerks is employed to take care of the rush of per
desiring to register immediately preceding elect
The office is open evenings at these times also.
special registrations are conducted in the various w
of the city. A voter can register and vote at any
tion by obtaining a certificate of residence signe
two property holders of the precinct in which he
sires to register. Twenty-five copies of the reg
lists are conspicuously posted in each voting prec
All registry lists are checked up by a police canva

Milwaukee system for conducting registrations
ections is recognized as far in advance of that
in any other city. The idea of a continuous,
lized registration originated here.

## f public buildings

the policy of the board of election commission-
use public buildings for polling places as much
sible. One hundred sixty-four polling places are
d in public schools and seventy-one are in booths
ally set up for that purpose. No booths are lo-
in places of business. Wherever it seems advis-
o the board, polling places may be located out-
f the boundaries of the precinct. This allows the
ishment of polling places of several precincts in
veniently located school or other public building.
ommission hopes that ultimately all polling booths
located in public buildings by making readjust-
in precinct lines and arranging the precincts
respect to public buildings.

## tration and voting

de from normal growth women's suffrage ined the number of registered voters from 84,000
fall of 1918 to 166,000 in the fall of 1920. Of
94,000 are men and 72,000 women giving a com-
ive voting strength of fifty-six per cent to the
nd forty-four per cent to the women for the entire
This number has now been increased to 168,000.
g the 1920 presidential election as a basis twenty-
per cent of the registered voters failed to exer-
heir privilege of voting. The women were more
gent than the men in this respect for thirty-six
nt of the women failed to vote as against fourteen
ent of the men.

## stricting

meet the limitation of six hundred actual voters
ne precinct, a redistricting of the city had to be
. The total number of precincts has been ined from 147 in 1918 to 235 in 1922. Preparation
change of precincts is made by the distribution
ps to each voter showing the precinct boundaries
the location of policing places.

## tions, 1922

o primary and two final elections were held during
ear. At the spring election, city attorney, a justice
e peace and constable were elected. The latter
officials have only nominal duties and perform
actual service. They are elected merely to comply
constitutional requirements. Bond issues of
0,000 for the widening of Cedar-Biddle street, of
0,000 for the construction of a viaduct over the
aukee river at Holton street and of $150,000 for
widening of the Folsom street bridge were ap-
ed by majorities ranging from three to six thou-
in a vote of approximately sixty thousand per-
The referendum on the proposal to allow the
ing of a public land fund tax not to exceed five-
s of a mill was defeated by a majority of 172 in
668 vote. This measure was first reported carried

Peter J. Koehler
William E. Brown

Mark H. Place, chief examiner
Herbert W. Cornell, assistant chief examiner.
R. C. Buelow, M. D., medical examiner

## Composition and duty

The board of city service commissioners cor
five persons, appointed, one each year, by the
Its duty is the examination and certification
fied persons for city positions and the hearing
plaints in regard to examinations, appointme
charges and suspensions from service.

## City employment

City employes get their positions either by
by appointment free from civil service restrict
by appointment from civil service eligible lis
elective officials consist of the mayor, member
common council and school board, the city tr
city comptroller and city attorney. Heads of
administrative departments and members of
administrative boards are appointed by the ma
ally subject to confirmation by the common
Administrative officers usually may appoint a
the city treasurer is allowed to make appoint
his office; and, in a few cases, boards may appo
chief administrative officer without reference
service. Teamsters for street work are also
from civil service. The appointment of teachers
by the school department, from qualified person
tically all other city employes are appointed f
service eligible lists. In cases where special
skill is required and upon the presentation of
the appointing officer showing a particular pe
ter fitted for the position than any other, exa
may be waived, but this does not happen in m
half a dozen cases in a year. Even common
are selected from eligible lists, secured after
physical and medical examination. Member
fire and police departments are under civi
though examinations for positions and hear
discharge or suspension in these departments
ducted by the fire and police commission.

## Number of city employes

It is an impossibility to make a count of
ployes which is correct at all times on accou
seasonal nature of a vast amount of city wo
ployment is always greater in the summer mo
in the winter months. A pay-roll check of em
the city comptroller's office shows that there
persons in the city employ during the first
January, 1923. Of these 2,984 were under th
civil service, 1,448 under civil service under
diction of the fire and police commission, 3,0
teaching service and 588 exempt from civi
Of the exempt positions 357 were drivers.

## Meeting and hearing of complaints

The commission held thirty-eight meeting
the year. Five appeals from discharges w
by the board. In all cases the charges of th
ment heads were sustained; in four cases the

eceived for these positions totaled 1,519. In cases were the examinations open to non- . In 100 instances the examination was for entrance to the service, in 21 cases original notional and in 9 instances promotional only. the most important examinations held were city plan engineer, deputy superintendent of and public buildings, supervisor of oral hy- d supervisor of property of the public museum. eight hundred applications were made for in the labor service, 196 certifications made to nt heads and 495 men received positions.

## l examinations

ard and its examiners have in every way at- to make examinations practical in their nature as would actually determine the fitness of ap- for the positions they were applying for. The of the strength of applicants for certain po- specially in the garbage incinerator was raised, a result, devices for testing strength, such as ps, pushing muscles and pulling muscles were Strength tests in the future will be taken ideration in selecting men for such positions. ing a city plan engineer, the applicants were e opportunity of actually platting a piece of lose proximity to Milwaukee from topographic pplied to them. Applicants for school janitors en into the boiler rooms of schools buildings to e their actual knowledge of that work. Nata- uperintendents were given swimming and life- ests.

## lists

ligible lists for approximately one-half of the tions were approved, but more than fifty old e abolished in December. As it will be neces- re-establish lists for many of these positions, desiring city employment will be given a wide opportunity.

## l condition of city laborers

e of many complaints a survey of the physical of laborers, who entered the service of the r to the institution of medical examinations by mission, was made during June, 1921. As a ver two hundred laborers were found to be physical standard now set by the commission. t common defects were such as could be largely l by the use of proper appliances. Orders to ach appliances and information concerning the to be derived therefrom were given. The facts sented to the common council but the communi- as placed on file without action. In October, re-examination of 150 laborers found below l revealed the fact that only 17 had complied request of the commission. Of the remaining were suffering from varicose veins or hernia eeded correction.

## BOARD OF FIRE AND POLICE COMMISSIONERS

Rybacki, chairman
mse

the board after competitive examination. The is assisted in its work by a chief examiner, b board participates in both the holding and mark examinations. Persons appointed to these se including the chiefs of the departments, hold positions for good behavior. Long service in po is the rule.

Besides conducting examinations the board check upon the discharge or suspension of men persons, suspended or discharged for any reason, soever, have a right to appeal their cases to it

## Examinations

During 1921 the commission gave ten examin to 376 applicants for appointment to the fire ar lice department.

## Revision of rules

The commission has also practically comple revision of its rules and regulations which will them very efficient, modern and up-to-date.

## CRIMINAL COURTS

August C. Backus, judge of the municipal court
George E. Page, judge of the district court
John W. Woller clerk of the municipal court

## Scope of authority

The municipal and the district courts are th factor, generally speaking, in the maintenance and order in the city of Milwaukee. It devolves them to pronounce judgment and punishment f lations of the city ordinances and state laws wher observance cannot be procured through other ag They are financed jointly by the city and cou Milwaukee.

The district court has jurisdiction to hear, tr determine all cases of violations of city ordinanc of offenses against the state law punishable by not exceeding one thousand dollars or impriso not exceeding one year. In cases of state offens which the penalties are greater, it has jurisdict conduct a preliminary examination and to dismis cases or bind them over for trial to the mu court if there is reason to believe that an offen been committed and that the accused is the perso committed it.

The municipal court has jurisdiction to hear, t determine all cases of offenses against the stat for which the penalties are greater than a fine thousand dollars or one year imprisonment and t appeals from the district court in cases for viol of the city ordinances or the lesser state offense

The clerk of the municipal court is charged wi making and custody of the records and the cal of these two courts and with various duties of ministrative and discretionary character, as an of the courts.

## Work, 1923

During 1922 there were 20,331 cases in the mu and district courts which required the attenda about 50,000 witnesses. The clerk collected $431, fines, penalties and costs and received $900,950

M. Niven
nd E. Stoelting
elius Corcoran
iam I. Greene
les W. O'Connor
Luke Hannifin
Doerfler, Jr.
P. Dietz
s Barr, secretary

## anization and budgetary control

he board of estimates, consisting of the mayor,
comptroller, city treasurer, city attorney, com-
ioner of public works, the president of the com-
council and the members of the finance committee
he common council, is charged with the duty of
ng up the annual city budget. The various de-
ment heads are required to submit their requests
ppropriations to the city comptroller who in turn
its them to the board. A sub-committee of the
l consisting of the mayor, commissioner of public
s and the chairman of the finance committee of
common council examines into the details of these
sts and makes recommendations to the board.

hen the budget is finally agreed upon by the board,
submitted to the council for approval. Both the
l of estimates and the common council hold public
ings. After adoption by the common council it
to the mayor, who may veto any item therein,
is approval

## pendent boards

park board, school board and board of industrial
tion have separate mill tax levies which makes it

city service commissioners also have mill t
but these provide a minimum levy only and ar
appropriation over this at the will of the
council. As these boards must have more
run their institutions and activities than the
levy provides, the common council has con
their entire appropriation.

## What the budget is

The budget is the fiscal program of the c
particular year. It contains a detailed stat
allowable maximum expenditures for the var
departments and of proposed bond issues. Ea
a distinct and separate appropriation which
exceeded or spent for any other purpose.

As the budget is prepared several months in
of actual expenditures and as some items w
to be too small and others too large, some
is provided for by allowing the board to make
justments as it deems advisable during the ye
out reference to the common council, except th
not allow the expenditure of funds for purj
which a fund has not already been include
budget. A contingent fund is set up under
council to meet unforeseen emergencies arisin
the year and to take care of needs not antic
the time of making the budget. Appropriati
the contingent fund require a three-fourths af
vote of the entire membership of the commor

## Taxation readjustment

The budget is adopted in two sections due to
that some of the city departments have the
raised in the tax levy of the year preceding

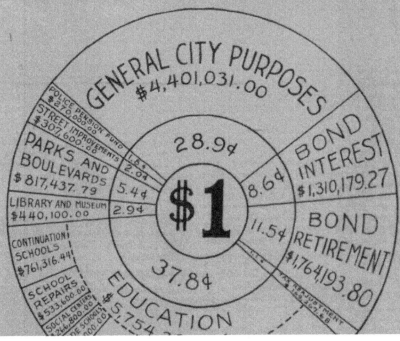

ll funds on a cash basis. Eventually a large
ion of the city revenue will be collected in ad-
f use without having placed a heavy burden
e tax payer by the change from collection of
fter expenditure by the city to collection before
ture. This fund has been allowed to accumu-
five years with the result that it was possible
r to finance the various activities of the park
rom this source. In the future the park board
ill be collected before expenditure. This com-
ie task of placing all of the independent boards
h basis. In addition the taxation readjustment
d a sufficient surplus to make it possible to
the board of election commissioners to a cash
so. As there is only one election in 1923, the
that department are just one-half of the ex-
e of a year in which there are two elections.
he transfer was much easier than it would
n last year or would be next year.

## sues

sed bond issues totaling $4,630,000 were placed
923 budget. These include $1,700,000 sewer
tion bonds, $1,000,000 grade crossing elimina-
ds, $750,000 school bonds, $500,000 harbor
200,000 auditorium bonds and $100,000 electric
bonds. Only such proportion of the grade
bonds as are actually needed will be issued.
usion of a greater amount in the budget is
ruling of the railroad commission that the
t be in a position to pay its share of the cost
evation or depression of the Chicago, Milwau-
St. Paul railway tracks on the northwest side
to make this work obligatory upon the
The sewer bond issue is for general sewer
ion and has no connection with the work
ewerage commission. Most of the money
is issue will be expended for the con-
of three sewers outside of the city limits
ng a comparatively small number of city resi-
contemplation of the needs of the outlying
when it is annexed to the city. The school
to be used for the construction of new school
and the acquisition of school sites. The audi-
nds, while an obligation upon the city, are to
rom the earnings of the Milwaukee auditorium.
to be used for necessary improvements and
The street lighting bonds are to be used
sions to the street lighting systems, much of
l be in newly annexed territory.

## budget

23 budget totals $25,464,000 as against budgets
,925 for 1922, of $28,274,840 for 1921 and of
3 for 1920. The increase over 1922 are dis-
as follows: independent boards, $700,000
istributed between the school board and the
industrial education, public debt charges
and the departments under the control of the
ouncil $500,000. These are offset to some ex-
decrease of $500,000 in the expenditures of
department.

causes of this change of policy is due to the fa
the school board has reached its statutory bon

The second half of the budget exclusive of
debt and taxation readjustment funds totaled $
000 of which $1,000 000 is for departments un
control of the common council, $760,000 for th
board which is to be financed from the taxatio
justment fund and $2,900,000 for the water
ment which is financed from its own earni
decrease of $500,000 in the expenditures of the
department is due to the fact that a greater
the cost of the Chambers street feeder main w
ried over from the 1922 budget.

There are 2,281 items in the 1923 budget v
from a one dollar allowance to the harbor mas
postage to one of $2,840,800 to the the school bo
salaries of elementary school teachers. Two
large items are $1,424,760 for salaries of pol
and $1,247,005 for salaries of the fire fighting f
the fire department. Over eight hundred items
budget are for sums over one hundred dollars o
while about seven hundred are for sums over one
and dollars.

## A glimpse into 1923

The cry of more streets and more alleys whic
raised last summer is reflected in an increa
$285,000 in this appropriation for this work. Th
item for this work was pared down being $240,0
low that of 1921 and $150,000 below that of
Greater activity in this work will be seen all ov
city as the result of this increase.

Greater efficiency in the disposal of garbage i
in the inclusion of an item of ninety thousand d
for the remodeling and enlarging of the garbage
erator. The research fund of the board of esti
will be used partly for the study of methods wh
the garbage collection systems can be improved.

The reorganization of the illumination burea
to the practical completion of the street lighting
struction program was brought about at the cl
the year. The Milwaukee river flushing plant is
automatically operated after April which involve
savings of salaries of a number of men.

The tax remission fund has been increased
six thousand to one hundred twenty thousand d
due to a large extent to the decision of the U
States supreme court exempting bank stock from
tion.

A new method for handling convention expendi
has been adopted. Hereafter all departments wi
to have representatives attend conventions will ha
appear before the committee on finance to give
reasons because convention appropriations have
omitted from departmental budgets and a co
council special fund of three thousand dollars for
purpose has been substituted.

Abutments to the Clinton and Pleasant s
bridges will cost ten thousand dollars each. Th
five thousand dollars will be spent for dredging

ties

The city comptroller is charged with the duties prescribing accounting methods and systems for the tral city government and its departments and of ing that the various agencies of government live hin their budgetary allowances. In order to do this ords are kept which show at all times the con- ions of the various funds. Not only must he see that artments live within their gross appropriations, he must also see that their money is spent in ac- dance with the segregated items in the budget. fore money can be paid out, the comptroller's sig- ure must be placed upon the city order to show t the expenditure is a proper charge against the r.

n the preparation of the budget all departments st submit requests for appropriations for the ap- aching year on forms and according to instructions nished by the comptroller's department. These re- sts are tabulated, checked carefully as to classi- tion and other essential details, and presented to the rd of estimates.

## trol of budgetary appropriations

he control of the budget is exercised through a inct accounting system under which two separate of accounts are maintained. One of these is the ropriation account and the other the special ac- nt for contracts and resolution appropriations ch together exceed thirty-five hundred in number. ch detail work is required in keeping the system each expenditure must be carefully checked up be- the comptroller's signature is affixed allowing payment from the city treasury.

udget appropriations for personal service are con- led through the adoption of ordinances and reso- ons specifying the number of employes in the ious departments and divisions of the city govern- t and their rate of pay.

upplies, materials and equipment in amounts of to exceed one thousand dollars are purchased by central board of purchases on requisition of the artment requiring the goods and such purchases not valid charges against the city until the comp- ler has countersigned the purchase thereof and re- ed, out of the fund appropriated therefor, a suf- nt amount to cover the purchase order when it mes due. Where a contract is let, the budget ropriation is charged with the amount of the tract and a reserve set up in the contract ledger.

here are items in the budget directly under the trol of the common council, such as the contingent d and common council special funds, which require ct action on the part of the common council in the n of a resolution, appropriating money from the d for expenditure by proper city official or direct- the issuance of a city order to be charged directly he fund.

he comptroller, in closing the books of the city at end of the year, provides reserves to take care of liability existing in the form of contracts, spe- resolutions of the common council and outstanding hase orders, so that payment of delayed matters

general understanding that money must n needlessly stimulates a conservation of creates a surplus. This surplus cannot be to another season but must be returned treasury. While the exact amount cann nitely ascertained before closing the books of the fiscal year, the practice exists of esti amount and using it to reduce the tax le current year. Any amount over the amc pated to be derived from this source is ap cash resources for the next year. A surpl 000 was accumulated from the surplus fu 1922 budget. Of this $700,000 was antici source of revenue to reduce the 1922 tax le mainder will be used as a source of rever 1923 budget.

## Revenue for 1923 expenditure

The estimated revenue for 1923 expenditu to about $24,000,000. Of this a sufficient carry the departments on a cash basis has in the 1922 levy while the amount necess raised by property taxation to carry the will be placed in the 1923 tax levy.

An analysis of the main source of city r 1920 shows that 67.9 per cent of the tota from the general property tax, 5.8 per cen income tax, 6 per cent from the water reven cent from licenses, and 18.9 per cent from eous sources. These proportions are prac rect to-day.

## Expenditures

The common council is frequently blam city's rapidly increasing expenditures, but mon council is not entirely to blame. In a ture of $22,500,000 for 1921, the common pended only $10,000,000 for the departments control. In terms of percentage the counc sponsible for 43.6 per cent of the total expe 1921 and the independent boards 34.1 per the payment of the principal and the inte public debt and the accumulation of the ta adjustment fund took 22.3 per cent of the

## Tax levy

The tax levy for 1923 was only seven n is one mill less than the sum which the city allowed and supposed it would be necessar due to the fact that the city's revenue from sources and unexpended departmental bala the previous year were much greater than when the preceding budget was made up.

The total tax levy of 1922 amounted t 193 of which $19,738,537 was upon real personal property and the balance upon in the property tax, $15,234,094, which is 77 p the total, was levied for city purposes and t

| e | Amount | Dollars Valuation | Dollar Tax |
|---|---|---|---|
| _____ | $19,738,537.28 | $29.15 | $1.00 |
| Wisconsin_ | 1,001,712.55 | 1.48 | $.051 |
| f Milwaukee | | | |
| l _____ | 2,757,298.75 | 4.07 | .139 |
| schools__ | 503,766.25 | .74 | .025 |
| debt_____ | 241,606.73 | .36 | .012 |
| [ilwaukee | | | |
| board____ | 4,992,968.02 | 7.37 | .258 |
| )l debt___ | 786,172.50 | 1.57 | .004 |
| n council_ | 4,708,631.00 | 6.94 | .238 |
| debt_____ | 2,288,200.47 | 2.99 | .116 |
| _____ | 817,437.79 | 1.21 | .042 |
| iation | | | |
| ls _____ | 761,316.44 | 1.12 | .038 |
| pension___ | 270,000.00 | .40 | .014 |
| library____ | 252,700.00 | .37 | .013 |
| museum__ | 187,400.00 | .28 | .010 |
| in read- | | | |
| ient _____ | 169,267.69 | .25 | .009 |

## s

al tax rate for 1922 was $29.15 per thousand f assessed valuation of property of which share was $22,50. The city rate is thirteen er than the 1921 rate. However, an increase nts in the county and state rate make the in combined rate only three cents less than A greater reduction had been anticipated, but e in personal property assessments of thirty ollars prevented this. Indications are that for next year will be somewhat higher on f the decrease of revenue from other sources ation.

## n tax rates

municipalities in Milwaukee county, West rth Milwaukee and Wauwatosa had a higher than the city of Milwaukee in 1921. West a rate of $35.84, North Milwaukee $34.42 and sa $30.00 per thousand dollars of assessed Milwaukee's rate was $29.18. Then came 27.72, Whitefish Bay $26,67, Shorewood 25.79, ining towns and villages had rates under

## is program

kee is leading American cities in becoming stomer and running its affairs on a strictly . The process includes the collection of city fore expenditure, direct financing of public ents by taxation and the elimination of pub- edness.

st step is being slowly accomplished by the readjustment fund. All of the independent id most of the small departments have now ed upon a cash basis. New activities are this basis from their beginnings. This pro- be slower in the future because departments rge expenditures as the health, police, fire and rks departments remain on the old basis.

suit of this Milwaukee is $1,275,000 nearer a basis than was generally realized.

## Direct financing

During the past ten years bond issues amountir over eight million dollars, which in former y would have been financed by bonds, have been fina from direct taxation resulting in a saving of al four million dollars in interest charges.

In conformity with this practice an issue of thousand dollars hospital bonds was eliminated included as a direct tax for 1923. The common c cil also authorized a special tax of two hundred t sand dollars for school construction purposes v hitherto have been financed through bond money. policy will be followed more closely to a greater tent in the future if the recommendations of the cial committee appointed by the superintenden schools to draw up a five year school building gram is followed.

## Personal service expenditures

An analysis of expenditures for 1921, which is stantially correct today shows that, excluding the of improvements, eighty per cent of the expendit of the independent boards and commissions seventy-two per cent of the expenditures of th partments under the control of the common co were for the personal services. Of the boards commissions the board of school directors, with eig five per cent and the library board with fifty-two cent, were high and low respectively in personal ice expenditures. In between these were the board with sixty-two per cent, the board of indus education with sixty and the museum board with s two per cent of these expenditures, devoted to purpose. Of the departments under the control of common council the police department spent ninety the fire department eighty-four, the building in tion bureau ninety-eight, the health department eig one, the bureau of street construction ninety-four bureau of street sanitation and garbage colle ninety-three, the water department thirty-three the illumination bureau thirteen per cent of t funds for this purpose.

## Legislative program

Milwaukee's enviable financial position is the sult of careful study of the city's financial prog Laws providing for the adoption of a segregated b et system, the creation of the taxation readjustr fund, the placing of purchasing on a cash disc basis and the substitution of direct taxation for issues in the financing of public improvements ar ready on the statute books. Laws providing for establishment of a debt amortization fund, the stitution of general funding bonds for bonds specific purposes, the future prevention of the ar pating of the income tax yield and the splitting of collections are before the 1923 legislature or in templation.

The passage of a general funding bond law make bond referendum turn upon the question of

to February 1, as tax collection in December
longer necessary because of the great extent to
h the city is on a cash basis. Taxes extended for
urrent year without this law total $1,200,000.

## lanation of statistical tables

e summary consolidated balance sheet is designed
ive a bird's eye view of the city's financial con-
n. It includes a functional division of the city's
unts in four different classes. The general acts are made up of resources derived from taxes
other current revenues which may be appropriated
eet current expenses and to pay liabilities incurred
ccount of current administration, operation and
tenance. The capital accounts are made up of
urces from the sale of bonds and from revenues
h may be used to pay liabilities incurred on ac-
t of the acquisition of permanent property. The
ing funds are all those resources held by the city
eserve for the amortization and redemption of the
cipal of the funded debt, and the payment of inst thereon. The special and trust accounts are
e resources which are held by the city in trust or
s capacity as special agent which may be used to
liabilities incurred in its capacity as trustee or
ial corporate agent. For the purpose of stating
cost of local service and improvements in one
unt, the part of such cost not assessable to the
tting property is included in this class of accounts.
he last item in the total column represents what
ht be entitled the present worth of the city except
it includes the total amount of the income tax to
collected while in reality the city receives only sev-
per cent of this revenue. The item is the total of
following amounts:

| | |
|---|---:|
| General revenue for 1923 from taxes | $ 718,656.00 |
| Income tax | 3,017,822.39 |
| Interest on street improvement as-sessments | 389,081.38 |
| Interest on bituminous resurfacing assessments | 7,121.42 |
| Departmental revenue for 1923 for taxes for independent boards | 6,016,465.46 |
| General surplus for 1923 | 57,976.26 |
| Departmental surplus for 1923 | 39,029.09 |
| Gifts and bequests | 8,240.00 |
| Capital account surplus—city's equity in its permanent property and equipment | 32,574,500.00 |
| | $42,828,892.00 |
| Less amount to be deducted from De-partmental revenue for 1923, for interest and principal due in 1923 on bonds of the historical museum which by law is payable out of the historical museum fund | 10,368.75 |
| | $42,818,523.25 |

The four supporting balance sheets support the
nmary statement. A great source of difficulty in
ding these is due to the fact that the collection of
es is not completed at the end of the fiscal year.

law for the interest upon
fund for the payment of the principal there

## City indebtedness

The city's debt at the end of the year was $2
and its debt limit $31,964,000 levying a m
$3,014,000 for the issuance of bonds during

The year 1922 has again established a hi
for issuance of Milwaukee bonds. A total o
000 have been authorized, of which $3,050,
been sold. The balance of the bonds will
he sold in the spring as there is no immedia
sity to have the cash on hand, and, in the r
the interest will be saved. Bonds issued
$500,000 school bonds; $200,000 electric lighti
$350,000 park bonds, for the purpose of ad
parks and inside playgrounds; $600,000 str
ing bonds, for the Cedar-Biddle project; $600,0
bonds, for the Cedar-Biddle street bridge;
harbor improvement bonds; $300,000 for loca
$150,000 for widening of the bridge at Folso
$2,500,000 city plan bonds, for the Cedar-Bi
center project; $240,000 grade crossing aboliti
for the city's portion of expense in connection
abolition of grade crossings on the Madison
of the North Western line. Of these issues
three remain unsold.

At the special election in April, an issue c
000 bridge bonds for the new Holton stree
was approved by the voters. While this ordi
been introduced and is pending in the commo
it is unlikely that there will be any defin
taken on it before 1923, and it is probable tha
of the viaduct will be considerably less than tl
voted for it. Whatever margin there will b
the amount of the bond issue and the actual
increase the net margin available to the city
issues.

## Policy

It appears that with the financing of the
disposal plant, the widening of Cedar a
streets, and several other large projects
the city has passed the period of high de
permanent improvements, and that the next
should see the demand for bond issues held
of approximately $2,500,000 annually. Mor
now the policy of the city, due to the activ
comptroller's office, to substitute direct ta
bond issues in many instances. In the past
eight million dollars worth of improvemer
under prior methods, would have been finance
issues, have been financed through direct ta

## Debt elimination

The commissioners are greatly interest
working out of a plan of debt elimination
allowed the expenditure of their funds for
of a plan of amortizing the public debt devi
comptroller's department. The result of
was submitted to a special committee appoir
council and consisting of the secretary to
deputy comptroller, secretary of the elec

or the city the interest from its own bonds.
est upon the fund will be used to augment
ipal. After the fund has reached three-
f the city's outstanding indebtedness, three-
f the annual interest accruals may be used
stallments and interest upon the public debt
ies due and to finance permanent public im-
ts which are now financed by bonds. Event-
s hoped that the fund will own all outstand-
f Milwaukee bonds and that thereafter there
o necessity of levying an annual tax for in-
l sinking fund purposes. While it is not an-
that this result will come about very quickly,
btedly will produce wonderful results in
e or thirty years. It is estimated that by
hree hundred thousand dollars in this fund
there will be an accrual of four million dol-
n years. There is approximately four hun-
sand dollars in the city treasury to start this

it is realized that seven cents of each dollar
taxes is used to pay interest charges on out-
bonds and over that amount for bond retire-
e importance of this measure can be seen.
of the tax rate the elimination of financing
provement bonds would mean a saving of
rs for interest charges and two dollars and
for installments on the principal on each one
dollars of assessed valuation.

The tax department makes all assessments upon
able real and personal property within the city
cept that belonging to railroads and public util
which is assessed by the state tax commission.
sides these sources of taxation, there is the stat
come tax which is assessed by the county assesso
incomes and the special assessments of benefits
damages for work done by the municipality along
upon the property of individuals which is assesse
the department of public works. The depart
keeps a complete set of records of all lots, bl
fractional lots or parcels of land in the city and
records necessary and convenient to carry ou
work. Personal property is assessed as of the
day of May while real property may be assessed
time between the first day of May and the meetin
the board of review consisting of the mayor,
clerk, tax commissioner and all assessors. This l
meets for the purpose of examining and adjustin
assessments which are properly brought before it.
city has been divided into seventeen districts fo
purpose of assessment for a number of years.
additional districts were created toward the clos
the year to take care of the increased work of
assessors and the territory newly annexed to the

## Assessed valuation; causes for decrease

The assessment roll for 1922 aggregated $677,
755, a decrease of $4,127,405 from the 1921 valua
This figure shows an increase of $4,180,135 on
estate valuations, of $9,763,910 on the valuation o

## COMPARATIVE BONDED DEBT OF AMERICAN CITIES

| City | Population Census 1920 | Gross Total Bonded Debt | Sinking Fund | Net Total Bonded Debt (Sinking Fund Deducted) | Per Capita Net Debt | R |
|---|---|---|---|---|---|---|
| k City | 5,621,151 | $1,730,160,385 | $644,563,884 | $1,085,596,501 | $193.13 | |
| | 2,701,705 | 113,353,800 | 736,000 | 112,617,800 | 41.68 | |
| hia | 1,823,779 | 250,165,550 | 54,859,535 | 195,306,015 | 107.09 | |
| | 993,739 | 142,159,930 | 10,429,274 | 131,730,656 | 132.56 | |
| | 796,836 | 123,101,524 | 15,249,595 | 107,851,929 | 135.35 | |
| (1) | 772,897 | 22,967,000 | 9,995,000 | 12,972,000 | 16.79 | |
| | 748,060 | 126,640,551 | 42,599,632 | 84,040,919 | 112.34 | |
| | 733,926 | 117,427,879 | 37,517,342 | 79,910,537 | 108.89 | |
| h | 588,193 | 58,201,900 | 3,481,200 | 54,720,700 | 93.03 | |
| cisco | 508,410 | 71,008,400 | 2,513,600 | 68,494,800 | 134.72 | |
| | 506,775 | 51,591,622 | 5,391,560 | 46,200,062 | 91.16 | |
| e | 457,147 | 27,750,500 | 3,478,923 | 24,271,577 | 53.09 | |
| on | 437,571 | 4,701,200 | 4,544,872 | 156,328 | 0.36 | |
| | 415,609 | 56,283,700 | 12,537,688 | 43,746,012 | 105.25 | |
| i | 401,247 | 100,113,231 | 23,796,745 | 76,316,486 | 190.20 | |
| lis | 380,582 | 37,512,106 | 3,012,434 | 34,499,672 | 90.65 | |
| ity, Mo | 324,410 | 21,683,000 | 6,169,785 | 15,513,215 | 47.82 | |
| | 315,652 | 55,144,500 | 572,058 | 54,572,442 | 172.89 | |
| lis | 314,194 | 18,264,850 | 1,033,262 | 17,231,588 | 54.84 | |
| | 295,750 | 28,716,020 | 3,032,917 | 25,683,103 | 86.84 | |
| | 258,288 | 28,246,200 | 2,855,148 | 25,391,052 | 98.30 | |
| | 256,369 | 22,783,600 | 136,596 | 22,647,004 | 88.33 | |
| | 243,109 | 31,532,969 | 5,713,660 | 25,819,309 | 106.20 | |
| e | 237,595 | 28,792,000 | 13,305,510 | 15,486,490 | 65.18 | |
| | 237,031 | 32,466,816 | 9,257,493 | 23,209,323 | 97.91 | |

a smaller output, causing a loss of $11,418,445 on class of property; second, the supreme court of United States rendered a decision last year in ch it held that the shares of stock in national ks cannot be taxed at a higher rate than moneyed ital is taxed in the respective states.

ince the enactment of the income tax law in 1911, eyed capital has been exempt from taxation in consin, except on its earnings. Since, under this sion, national bank stock is placed in the same s, it becomes exempt from taxation. However, the onal banks, not desiring to avoid the payment of tax, expressed a willingness to a partial assess-t of their bank stock, namely in an amount as ld yield a tax equivalent to what they would be ired to pay were they subject to income taxation. reduced assessment, however, which has been made inst the national banks resulted in a loss of $7,515,-on this class of property.

oth of the causes above mentioned were beyond control of the taxing authorities, the first being omic in its nature, while the latter was a matter ourt construction of an old federal law.

### rease of value of automobile

s another instance of falling values, the assess-t of automobiles may be cited. In 1921 this de-tment assessed 30,485 automobiles, trucks and orcycles at a total valuation of $18,420,805, averag-$604 per machine. In 1922, 36,970 machines were ssed at $17,526,655, an average of $474 per auto-ile. Although there were 6,485 more machines

Over 190,000 separate assessments were arriving at the total assessment roll. properties each have an assessed valuatio $500,000. Of these the Plankington Arcad is high with a valuation of $4,065,000; then First Wisconsin National Bank Building wi 000, the International Harvester Company with $2,897,400; the Majestic building a Theater with $2,300,000 and the Northweste Life Insurance Company property with Sixteen properties are valued between on million dollars each.

### Opposition to tax legislation discrimina cities

Toward the end of the year the commissic staff member of the citizen's bureau of mu ficiency made a seventeen hundred mile visiting all of the principal cities of the sta purpose of bringing about an agreement s governing authorities to oppose attempts of legislature to levy increase tax burdens county or highway purposes which would n that a share of the money raised in the cit be returned to them for use in local street co and repair.

This trip resulted in a mutual understa tween the legislative committee of the leagu consin municipalities and a like committe county boards association of the state relativ way and automobile legislation, and their de are embodied in a satisfactory bill which is the legislature for its consideration.

## COMPARATIVE ASSESSMENT AND TAX DATA, UNITED STATES CITIES

| Name of City | Area Square Miles | Population 1923 Census Estimate | Total Amount of Assessed Valuation | Per Cent of Basis of Assessment | Ta per fo Pu |
|---|---|---|---|---|---|
| York | 314.7 | 5,927,625 | $10,460,603,675 | 100 | $ |
| ago | 192.8 | 2,886,121 | 1,666,215,416 | 50 | |
| adelphia | 128.0 | 1,922,788 | 2,919,804,723 | 100 | |
| roit | 82.3 | 995,668 | 1,954,184,000 | 100 | |
| eland | 56.0 | 888,519 | 1,569,306,730 | 100 | |
| Louis | 61.3 | 803,853 | 984,257,140 | 100 | |
| ton | 47.8 | 770,400 | 1,677,861,774 | 100 | |
| imore | 92.9 | 773,580 | 1,103,024,580 | 100 | |
| Angeles | 365.6 | 666,853 | 915,421,338 | 50 | |
| sburg | 45.9 | 613,442 | 868,177,930 | 100 | |
| Francisco | 46.5 | 539,058 | 857,464,045 | 50 | |
| falo | 42.0 | 536,718 | 647,095,740 | 100 | |
| waukee | 26.9 | 484,595 | 677,070,755 | 100 | |
| vark | 23.2 | 438,699 | 592,637,203 | 100 | |
| cinnati | 71.1 | 406,312 | 739,997,200 | 100 | |
| Orleans | 196.0 | 404,575 | 482,690,265 | 100 | |
| neapolis | 53.0 | 409,125 | 274,126,900 | a | |
| sas City | 59.5 | 351,819 | 426,761,130 | 100 | |
| ttle | 94.0 | 315,312 | 232,851,469 | 50 | |
| anapolis | 43.6 | 340,882 | 598,826,710 | 100 | |
| ey City | 19.2 | 209,034 | 465,509,926 | 100 | |
| hester | 31.6 | 317,867 | 340,042,563 | 100 | |

. Dudgeon
rbach
iicki
. Reynolds
Schumacher
. Callahan, purchasing agent
Nicholson, secretary and chief buyer

## ion

tral board of purchases has been in charge
sing supplies and materials for the city
. It is composed of representatives of the
uncil, the departments under its control and
pendent boards. A staff of buyers is main-
general city purchasing while purchasing
dependent boards is made through buyers
by the respective boards.

## procedure

rd is, by statute, required to make all pur-
ounting to one thousand dollars or more by
ntract to the lowest responsible bidder un-
c permission to do otherwise is given by the
uncil by a two-thirds majority vote. More-
common council is very reluctant to deviate
practice of requiring formal bids unless it
rly shown that an actual saving can be made
sing upon the open market or unless the
e otherwise benefited as by the standardiza-
achinery. As far as possible all purchases
on specifications. A file of one thousand
logues and a record showing all previous
ept in the department. A stock of supplies
nonly asked for is kept in the department

## of 1922

rchases made by the department for 1922
to $2,700,000 dollars. Materials, supplies
e furnished on twenty thousand requisitions
to $1,500,000 while twenty-three formal con-
e let for materials and services valued at
Cash discounts amounted to twenty-one
dollars which is an increase of ten thou-
rs over 1921. In making the purchases the
with fifteen hundred vendors and received
ed quotations on three thousand items. The
handled forty-seven hundred requisitions
rd supplies amounting to ninety thousand
ts annual inventory at the end of the year
stock on hand valued at fifty thousand dol-
mpared with a stock of sixty-two thousand
the beginning.

gest contracts of the year were one amount-
6,000 for coal for the city buildings, one of
or water pipe and one of $240,000 for ce-
he sewerage disposal plant. A large amount
ed fire equipment was purchased during the
s included four Seagrave pumpers, one squad
l one chemical wagon. The latter two were
which were remade and converted at fire
t shop.

three to four and one-half cents per gallon. The ta
will be placed along the railroad tracks. Tank
will deliver directly to them and a tank wagon wil
used to hand gasoline to the various city garages.

## CITY TREASURER

John I Drew, city treasurer
Martin McLaughlin, deputy city treasurer.

## Duty

The city treasurer is charged with the duty of
ceiving all payments to the city, including tax p
ments, to keep an account of the same and to pay
city monies when properly authorized to do so.

## Tax bills

Personal property, income and surtax bills
mailed to tax payers early in December. The tax p
er who is subject to both income and personal prop
taxation can offset one against the other, that is
the greater of the two. Owners of real property n
call for their tax bills personally or request them
mail because the tax assessed against the prop
rather than the person and ownership is not recor
on the tax bills on account of frequent changes.

## Tax collection

Collection of the tax levy begins the first of Dec
ber and continues until the end of the following J
uary. The vast number of persons who call for tl
tax bills and make personal payments necessit;
the installation of temporary booths and counters
the main floor of the city hall. On account of
vast number of tax accounts paid by check mailed
the department, another month is necessary for tal
care of mail collections. Time for payment of ta
is usually extended by the council for this per
Delinquent personal property tax accounts are t
turned over to the police for collection. Extension
time for payment for six months with six per
interest is granted to those who wish this convenie
About three million dollars worth of taxes were
tended this year.

## Tax sales

Sale of unpaid tax bills begins the first of Fel
ary. These bills which have not been paid or
which no arrangement has been made to extend p
ment are sold to the highest bidder. After purch;
of tax bills of a property have been made for tl
successive years, the purchaser can obtain title to
property. Any tax bills which have been sold may
recovered within the three years by payment of t
face value plus interest charges.

## Receipts

The total receipts of the city treasury for 1922 v
$93,738,164. About fifty per cent of this repres
withdrawal from banks. Other large receipts inc
$18,544,170 from real and personal property ta
$2,175,021 from the income tax, $1,674,323 from
extensions, $893,108 from the income surtax.
receipts from fees, licenses and permits totaled

million dollars deposits in banks, six million for
ed States certificates of indebtedness. The de-
s in banks are of temporary short-term nature

lic school system totaled $6,611,828 of which
was for the repair of school buildings and $92
construction work.

# PUBLIC WORKS AND PUBLIC UTILITIES

## DEPARTMENT OF PUBLIC WORKS

nd E. Stoelting, commissioner
d McKeith, deputy commissioner
ge F. Staal, city engineer
ry P. Bohmann, waterworks
uel Cutler, bridges and buildings
les O. Davis, street sanitation and garbage collection
nas E. Hayes, sewers
ard Ilgner, electrical service
inand Krieger, power plants
ge R. Stolz, plumbing inspection
les J. Van Etta, street construction and repair

## anization and duties

e range of activities of the department of public
s is the most extensive of any department under
control of the common council. It includes all
ral city work in connection with street improve-
, street cleaning, garbage and ash collection,
rworks, construction and maintenance of bridges
buildings, street lighting, power plants and sewer
ruction, except that of intercepting sewer system
the construction of the sewerage disposal plant
h are under the jurisdiction of the sewerage com-
on.

e commissioner of public works, who is in charge
e activities of this department, is also a member
e board of estimate and the subcommittee of the
i, the central board of purchases and the board
iblic land commissioners.

e mayor's appointee to the position of com-
oner of public works was confirmed by the coun-
; its charter meeting in April.

## ganization

number of changes were made by the board of
ates and common council in the organization of
epartment to secure greater efficiency or greater
my. Among these were the merging of the con-
tion and lighting divisions of the illumination
u, the motorization of the plumbing service which
it possible to reduce the number of inspectors,
he elimination of one operating shift at the high
ce pumping station of the water works. Legisla-
authorizing the appointment of a superintendent
arbage collection and disposal is being sought
the state legislature.

## ulting architect

e of the new commissioner's first moves was to
a the accentance of Mr. William Schuchardt, pres.

sustaining, and the special assessment work
into account, it is safe to say that it has contr
expenditure of more money than any other
ment. The waterworks budget alone totaled
000 for 1922. The largest items in the 192
were $530,000 for street construction and
$465,000 for ash collection, $740,000 for the
nance of public bridges and buildings, $330
street lighting, $250,000 for the operation
plants, $250,000 for garbage collection, $11
sewer construction and $80,000 for engineeri
ices.

## Contracts and permits

The department entered into three hund
nineteen contracts covering public works activ
totaling $3,500,000. Approximately one mil
lars of this however was for the constructio
Chambers street feeder main of the waterwo

Over ten thousand paid permits, bringing
enue of twenty thousand dollars, and seven
free permits were issued allowing work to
upon or otherwise affecting the public highwa
paid permits included 3,100 for the excavation
for the deposit of building materials and 2
laying house and storm drains.

## Special assessments and condemnations

The total amount of work for which specia
ments were included in the 1922 tax roll appr
$1,200,000, an increase of $120,000 over 19
amount of assessable street and alley impr
totaled $950,000 and of street resurfacing $96
only part of this was placed upon the tax rol
the practice to divide each assessment in s
parts and levy one-sixth of it annually so
burden will not be felt too heavily by the
owners. An interest rate of six per cent is
by the city on the deferred payments.

Damages amounting to $205,000 were awa
the taking of property in opening six streets
alleys, of which $112,000 was assessed, as
against the abutting property and $93,000 ch
to city funds. The largest projects were the
of Martin street from the Milwaukee river
Water street, with benefits assessed against t
erty owners amounting to $87,000 and amounts
able to city funds totaling $40,000 and of T
street from Twenty-seventh to Hopkins str
benefits assessed to the property owners of $5
costs chargeable to the city totaling $48,000.
vacating of all or parts of five alleys and o
benefits were assessed, amounting to $700 and
awarded amounting to $45. The damages

es; flushed 368 feet of sewers and inspected
s of sewers. The new sewers in the Layton
ct between Twenty-seventh, Lincoln, West-
abst avenues were completed but is not in-
the total for 1922 because they were not
n the tax roll. The department installed
ic ejector at Pabst and Western (Thirtieth)
raise the sewage from the sewers of this
d also at Bradford and South Shore bath-
s to divert the sewage previously discharged
ke to the main sewers in these districts.

## nstruction

eet construction for 1922 was less than for
o a large cut in the budget appropriation
rk. Nevertheless, a great amount of work
plished with the money allow d. Eight and
ineal miles of pavement, including six miles
one and a seventh-eighth miles of cement
nd one-fifth of a mile each of granite and
block were constructed. The standard
alt paving amounted to 120,000 square
phalt resurface to 25,000 square yards,
resurface to 200,000 square yards, ce-
crete to 37,000 square yards, granite
8,000 square yards and hard sandstone
ards. The largest asphalt jobs of the year
he paving of South Bay street from Kinnie-
Lincoln avenue, of Center street from Sher-
vard to Fifty-first street, Lake street from
to Richards and the resurfacing of Oakland
m Folsom place to Edgewood avenue. Fif-
ne-third lineal miles of cement concrete was
alleys. All new work was done by contract
ir work was done by city labor. Over two
en and teams were employed daily in the
eason by contractors. The city employed
tely one hundred fifty men. Thirty men
oyed by the city to inspect the paving jobs
contractors

3 program provides for more work and
onomy than in previous years. Stone crush-
nery has been installed in the county air-
from which crushed stone will be furnished
l hauled to the places where it is needed by
instead of being purchased from private
More rigid inspection will be made of pav-
acceptance of work by the city. Less as-
be laid than in previous years and specifica-
asphalt paving will be opened up to allow
n between natural and petroleum asphalts.
have been barred from city work for a
years. More cement concrete street and
will be done than ever before.

n the 1923 session of the legislature, the
f an act was secured which will allow the
e of part of the county's share of the state
ax upon the main traffic arteries of cities
county. Hitherto, although the great pro-
this money was raised within the city of
none of it could be expended for highway
while the abutting property was valued at
twenty dollars per foot. Under the new

## Streets,

| | | | |
|---|---|---|---|
| Standard sheet asphalt | 27 | 121,329.42 | 3.7 |
| Eight traffic asphalt | 1 | 959.85 | 3.6 |
| Asphalt resurface | 3 | 24,801.82 | 2.5 |
| Cement concrete | 7 | 37,079.43 | 2.0 |
| Granite block | 3 | 7,934.03 | 5.0 |
| Hard sandstone | 1 | 2,897.47 | 5.7 |
| Creosote block | 1 | 337.97 | 5.5 |
| | | Lin. feet | |
| Cement curb and gutter | 2 | 3,474.60 | .8 |

## Repair,

| | Yards | Per y |
|---|---|---|
| Asphalt | 81,313 | $0.7 |
| Brick | 8,603 | 1.3 |
| Sandstone | 3,042 | 1.4 |
| Granite | 6,143 | 1.4 |
| Creosote block | 10,165 | 1.7 |
| Macadam resurface | 202,711 | .0 |
| Macadam repair | 12,428 | .8 |
| Limestone | 101 | 1.3 |
| Concrete | 551 | 1.9 |
| Creosote block | 1,977 | 2.5 |

## Street cleaning and minor street repair

The work of keeping the five hundred city street
a clean, sanitary and usable condition is very extens
especially during the warm months of the year. T
must be swept, either by hand or by machine;
pavements must be washed; the macadam streets n
be oiled; and the catch basins must be cleaned. A la
amount of motor equipment is necessary to do
work properly. In the winter snow must be remo
During 1922, 92,000 cubic yards of sweepings v
removed from the city streets at a cost of $240,
Approximately 45,000,000 gallons of water were
for sprinkling and 80,000,000 gallons more for fl
ing at a cost for both activities of $85,000 which
cluded water and teaming. One hundred and tw
miles of streets were oiled during the summer mon
This is a greater mileage of streets treated in
fashion since 1919; in 1921 only forty miles of str
were oiled. Approximately 640,000 gallons of oil
used for this purpose and the cost was $125,000, p
tically all of which was assessable. Thirteen t
sand cubic yards of material was removed from c
basins. Although the winter season of 1922 was
mild, it was necessary to spend over $20,000 for s
removal.

The bureau does a great deal of minor and em
ency street repair work such as is necessitated
cave-ins and washouts, repairing defective gutters
alley crossings, patching of waterbound macadam r
ways to place them in condition for oiling, and rep
ing of street crossings. During 1922 between six
seven miles of dirt road were maintained with g
ing machinery and cinders, and over one hundred
alleys improved with cinders to make them pass
for automobiles. Sixteen macadam alleys were constructed at a cost of seventy-five cents per square y
and their cost assessed to the property. A road
pair outfit was used to make substantial repairs w
a street was becoming rutted. A stone crusher

ator for the loading and handling of garbage.
y of the collection districts is also being made.
e two ton trucks were purchased and operated as
age collecting units. Eighty thousand loads of
age, amounting to 47,000 tons, were collected dur-
he year at a cost of $253,000. The records show
over five thousand tons of garbage were collected
ach of the months of August, September and
ber, forty-seven hundred tons in July, forty-two
red in June, from thirty-four to thirty-nine hun-
tons in May, November, and December, and three
sand tons or below for the balance of the months
ie year. A total of 465,000 cubic yards of ashes
rubbish were collected at a cost of $468,000. The
ction and removal of 3,570 dead animals was made
collector, hired for that purpose.

## nbing

l plumbing and drain connection work in the city
be approved by the bureau of plumbing. A per-
ent field force is maintained to inspect plumbing
house drain inspection. In addition to the per-
ent force, other inspectors are stationed on house
and water service connections installed from the
in the street to the curb preceding permanent
t paving.

ie unprecedented number of permits issued dur-
he year reflects the unusual building activity of
past season. The number of inspections was ten
cent over 1921, the previous record year. The field
made 15,198 plumbing and 17,510 drain inspec-
which resulted in 1,962 rejections of plumbing
747 of drain installation which is less than one
cent of total inspections. Over 6,300 plans were
oved. A total of 1100 sanitary, 800 storm drains
1200 water connections were installed to the curb
iring an aggregate of over six miles of trench
A decrease in the number of inspectors from
to six was made late in the year. Investigation
ed that these men were spending sixty per cent
ieir time riding street cars from one job to an-
By providing automobiles the time spent in
ling will be reduced to twenty or thirty per cent.
sion of the plumbing code continued by a com-
e of interested parties. This code is now ready
n process of publication.

number of changes have been made in its require-
s. A charge based upon the number and classi-
on of fixtures to be levied in the same manner
uilding permit fees has been accepted as the
is of distributing the cost of the office.

## er plants

e power plants operated by the department in-
the refuse incinerator, the incinerator power
, the Milwaukee river flushing station, the Kin-
nnic river flushing station and the Menomonee
special sewage pumping station on the Jones
d.

proximately fifty-nine thousand tons of garbage

and the furnishing of a sufficient amount of
supply the plant. With an adequate supply o
no coal will be required to operate the plant.
moval of ashes from the plant to the dump i
to be quite a problem on account of the increa
tance between the two.

Power for the operation of the Milwauk
flushing station was furnished from the in
power plant as in previous years. Plans for
tinuance of the operation of this station pr
the reduction of its operating force from 8 i
men during the coming season. In complia
orders from the health department, there was
ing during periods of heavy south and sc
winds in order to protect the water works int
contamination.

The maintenance of the Jones Island sewag
ing station was transferred to the sewerage
sion during the year. The city will pay the co
twenty-five hundred dollars a month until i
mantled when the pumping machinery of the
plant will be placed in commission.

# BRIDGES AND PUBLIC
# BUILDINGS

## Construction and repair work

No large or spectacular construction work
gun during 1922. While a number of proje
under consideration, lack of funds, legal tar
proceedings and the necessity of acquiring
sites by the slow process of condemnation
all large undertakings. Many of the ground
lay have been overcome, and, as a result,
see a number of projects started. The most i
of these is the long desired, long delayed Sta
bridge. Bonds were voted for this project t
ago, but rising costs and the insistance of the
government upon certain changes in the pla
it necessary to secure the approval of an a
issue of bonds. The original issue was for
the issue approved by the electorate in the Ap
election is for $280,000. Other work in conte
for 1923 is the widening of the Folsom stree
the paving of the American avenue and Cleve
enue bridges and the North avenue viaduct ap
and the construction of the nurses' home of t
View hospital, the Prairie street natatorium,
ket building and comfort station at Thirt
Center streets and the Grand avenue bridge
station.

The normal amount of repair work was
lished. Principal among these was the recon
of the north abutment of the Racine stree
roadway and walk repairs to the Sixteenth st
duct and miscellaneous fender piling repai
Racine street bridge work was necessitated thr
failure of the abutment resulting in the en
north span dropping into the river.

## eaches

e hundred thirty-five thousand people are
o have attended the McKinley and South
ing beaches. This is only five thousand less
921 attendance, which, considering the cool
ould seem to indicate that more people are
he public bathing beaches than ever before.
does not include the number of bathers at
beach nor the number who come to the
utomobile in bathing costume. Lake bath-
ed to a four month season and the greater
s in 1922 was included in July and August
one hundred and ten thousand of the total
patronized the beaches.

rsion of sewage from the bathing beaches
plished during the year by the construction
to pump the sewage up into the regular
rs.

## ns

en hundred and fifty thousand persons at-
seven public natatoriums. There was very
ence in the number of persons attending any
se as the attendance in each case hovered
one hundred thousand mark. The records
seventy-five per cent of the total attend-
men and boys.

## icles

ber of motor vehicles owned by the city
Seventy-five Fords of different kinds,
Seagrave fire trucks and pumpers, twenty-
y-Davidson motorcycles, nineteen horse-
tor operated flushers, sixteen Diamond T
rteen Dodges, eight Kelly-Springfield trucks,
ce-Arrow police department cars are in-

he year the seventy-one cars, operated out
licipal garage, made runs totaling 350,000
average cost of ten and eight-tenths cents
the transaction of city business.

r of changes were made in the office ar-
in the city hall during the past year.
most important of these were the removal
rage commission to the old Hartford hotel
w owned by the city, the transfer of the
ublic land commissioners offices to the sev-
the doubling of the space alloted to the
building inspection by the removal of
nspection bureau to offices vacated by the
eights and measures, who was transferred
house on the second ward market grounds,
rrangement of the offices of the department
orks.

## ELECTRICAL SERVICE

### system

four hundred candle-power, which are used in
suspension units at street intersections in reside
districts; nineteen hundred are two hundred and f
candle-power; thirteen hundred are six hund
candle-power; and over five hundred are one th
sand candle-power.

## Character of lighting

Milwaukee is the first large city in the United Sta
to have its streets entirely lighted by gas-filled
candescent tungsten lamps. This was brought ab
by the practical completion of the municipal system
1921, by the conversion of the fifteen hundred
units to electric units and the replacement of the
maining 275 arc lamps with the new type incandesc
lamp units in 1922. The gas units were installed
1915 with the idea of having a dual system so th
in case of interference with the electric lighting s
tem, the gas lighting system could be depended u
to furnish some light. The replacement of arc w
incandescent lamps is important because it indicate
general change in the city's electric lighting syst
since the time of the commencement of elect
lighting.

## Conversion of gas units

While the cost of converting the gas units was o
one hundred dollars per unit, the result is grea
economy in maintenance charges and better lighti
There is an annual saving of eight dollars per lamp
electrical over gas units even after a charge of ei
per cent is added to cover amortization and inter
charges on the investment necessary to make
change. Night outages on the gas units averaged
per cent as compared to two and one-half on
electric units. Moreover, tests made on the stre
show one hundred per cent more light under the el
tric as compared with gas lighting.

The conversion was accomplished with great d
culty as it was necessary to install thousands of f
of cable and to completely readjust the existant lig
ing circuits to accommodate the additional load wi
out suspending operation of any part of the syste
As an instance of this the breaking up of the dem
stration circuit installed in 1915 in the downto
section of the city. This necessitated the breaking
this circuit in as many as eight places during a d
the making of the proper connections with other
cuits and the placing of all circuits in operation
night time.

## Records

During the coming year a set of installation rec
maps, showing the exact location of all undergrou
and overhead equipment, will be started so that
element of guesswork in locating equipment will
unnecessary in the future.

Lamp records are kept to record the life of lam
in service so as to determine the desirability of
various types and kinds of lamps, and to elimin
troubles brought to light from study of these recor
Very successful work has been done in eliminat
outages during the heavy storms. It is also possi
by this means to indicate the quality of purchases a
to find out whether they are up to the standard

## ffic control

ontinued research has been carried on in the elec-
al shop and testing laboratory to perfect various
lic devices which will be simple in construction and
:omical in operation and upkeep with a view to
:dardizing equipment throughout the city and ob-
ing it at a reasonable cost.

xperimental devices have been installed at several
et intersections and are giving satisfaction. One of
e consists of the four posts bearing "go" and
p" signals to be set at each corner of the street
rsection back of the inner line of the sidewalk. The
antage of the devices is that their cost is very
ll, that they are out of the center of the street and
not be knocked over so readily and that they stop
lic back of the sidewalks keeping them clear for
estrian traffic which can move in the direction of
vehicular traffic expeditiously and without inter-
nce or danger. Another is a traffic button for
center of the street which is inexpensive in opera-
and which can be synchronized with the traffic
lights.

he city now owns two self regulating traffic devices,
a ground device and the other an overhead device.
eral others have been installed on the city streets
he inventors. A number of mushroom lights were
alled during the year bringing the total number in
ration up to 119. Most of the traffic devices are
ected to the street lighting circuits.

undreds of "stop" signs were erected during the
year along the arterial highways and are being
ntained by this bureau.

he intensifying of illuminating along arterial high-
s is being considered so as to make possible the
ming of headlights and to allow motorists to trav-
these streets with the greatest comfort and safety
edestrian traffic and to themselves.

## ENGINEERING

### ineering supervision

ll civil engineering activities of the department of
lic works are in charge of the city engineer sub-
to the direction of the commissioner of public
ks except those engineering problems which con-
the waterworks, of which the city engineer has
rvisory authority independent of the commissioner.
work of the bureau includes the preparation of
mates of the cost and the drawing of plans for
lic improvements and the drafting of specifications
materials.

### p work

ompiling of quarter section maps of the city has
steadily going on. The original number of such
s numbered one hundred twenty-five, but these
s are constantly being revised to conform to the
latest changes. Information was gathered during
year, and rough plats were made for sixty-seven
quarter sections which will be completed as the
rtunity presents itself. Fourteen new quarter

in Milwaukee and the suburban communities
permit a much better interlacing of these sy

Plans were prepared for about eight miles
Extensive studies were made to determine ho
facilities could be furnished for the territory
annexed to the city and construction of sewe
started in 1923 to provide for these areas.

The sewer that discharged into the lake
Point pumping station has been diverted
North avenue sewer. Automatic ejectors
installed to pump the sewage. In a like m
sewage from the South Shore park pavilion
pumped into the intercepting sewers at Ru
and Superior street. The construction of
sewer for the Keefe avenue sewer east of
seventh street is well under way. When co
will relieve the flooding of the neighboring

### Grade separation

Late in the year the Northwestern railway
task of eliminating grade crossings along its
division tracks on the extreme south side o
between First and Forest Home avenues. '
was ordered by the Wisconsin railroad comi
1917 but never undertaken on account of th
construction during the war and unsettled
at its close. The right of way is now bein
from grade at First avenue so that the tra
passing over that street will pass under a
for nearly three miles returning to grade
Thirty-seventh avenue where the county wil
street to pass under the tracks in a subway
distance only nine streets will continue a
tracks; the remaining streets will end at e
of the railway right of way. Before the jo
pleted which will not be before 1924, more th
million cubic yards of excavation will have b
and more than fifty thousand cubic yards
poured into the retaining walls and bridge s
When completed all the dangerous railway
on the south side will have been eliminated.

The railroad is bearing the expense of exca
right of way and building abutments and bri
the city is paying for grading approaches t
building retaining walls and for excavat
avenue from Cleveland nearly to Oaklahom
The entire project will cost about one and
million dollars of which the city will pay
hundred thousand dollars.

Two contracts were let during the year, o
depression of First avenue from Cleveland a
point 225 feet south of the center line
street and the other for the elevation of Mi
Eighth avenues from Cleveland avenue to
Work started on First avenue in July and
avenue in November. Work on Midland a
not be started until Eighth avenue is opened
The construction work on First avenue c
4,400 cubic yards of earth excavation, 1,600 c
of uniform concrete retaining wall, 3,700
of backfill around retaining walls, removin
laying the water mains, removing the pavem
sidewalk and curbing and the construction
crete arch above an eighty-four inch sewer.

bering and street nomenclature committee.
ment of house numbers under the plan pro-
he commission and adopted by the common
be made by the city engineer's office.

## 'AGE OF WATER IN RIVERS*

|  | Highest | Lowest | Mean |
|---|---|---|---|
| y --------- | —1.02 | —2.08 | —2.028 |
| ry ------ | —0.8 | —2.8 | —1.989 |
| ---------- | —1.3 | —2.5 | —1.704 |
| ---------- | —0.7 | —1.9 | —1.232 |
| ---------- | —0.35 | —0.9 | —0.686 |
| ---------- | 0.0 | —1.0 | —0.576 |
| ---------- | —0.2 | —1.5 | —0.491 |
| t --------- | —0.2 | —1.0 | —0.600 |
| iber ----- | —0.4 | —1.2 | —0.825 |
| r --------- | —0.7 | —1.7 | —1.117 |
| ber ------ | —0.9 | —2.1 | —1.544 |
| ber ------ | —1.6 | —2.85 | —2.155 |
| ---------- | +1.6 | —2.4 | —0.895 |
| ---------- | +2. | —2.2 | +0.361 |
| ---------- | +0.7 | —1.9 | —0.339 |
| ---------- | +1.3 | —0.6 | +0.173 |
| ---------- | +3.0 | —0.8 | +0.086 |
| ---------- | —0.6 | —2.9 | —1.809 |
| ---------- | +0.4 | —1.9 | —1.690 |

ables, compiled from daily readings, show
of water levels on the lake and rivers and
and extremes. These elevations refer to the
line as a base, which is 581.22 feet above
t New York city, assuming the level of the
river as it was in March 1836 as a base.

## WATERWORKS

### ›ply

ee's municipally owned and operated water-
›lies water to the cities of Milwaukee and
the villages of Shorewood, North Milwau-
Milwaukee and Whitefish Bay, to the county
in the town of Wauwatosa and to a num-
ividual consumers in the towns of Green-
Milwaukee and Wauwatosa.

chigan is the source of the entire water
ie intake in service at present is known as
d avenue intake, and consists of a concrete
l of twelve feet internal diameter and 6,553
yth terminating in an octagonal submerged
, 86 feet 7 inches long diameter, 80 feet
ster and 12 feet in height in 67 feet depth
The lake shaft which connects with the in-
f the tunnel is twelve feet in diameter. The
his shaft is one hundred fifty feet below city
ie submerged timber intake crib of the tun-
ed about five miles from the entrance of the
he capacity of the intake is approximately
ed twenty million gallons in twenty-four
velocity of three feet per second. It was
supply not only the present North Point
ation, but also a future station which will
on the Milwaukee river near Chambers
e known as the Riverside pumping station.

during 1922 was $2,087,163. The net income of
department, over and above operations, maintenar
depreciation and interest on bonded indebtedness,
cluding new construction and equipment purchas
was $1,308,422.

The cost of operation and maintenance for the y
1922, excluding depreciation, was $581,154.47, a
crease of $11,660.56 from 1921.

New construction work, paid for out of the ea
ings of the department and which increased the va
of the plant, totaled $1,301,927.11.

Since 1913 no bond issues have been required, as
expenditures have been paid out of the earnings. T
sum of $225,000 of the earnings of the department w
transferred to the general city fund toward reduc
the general tax. Since 1892 the sums transferred
this manner aggregate $3,767,965, which exceeds
sum raised by tax levy in support of the waterwo
before the department was self-sustaining by $1,89
426.

The book value of the waterworks, less depred
tion written off, is $12,109,862.25 with a bonded d
of $150,000 after deducting the sinking fund on ha

### Pumpage

The total pumpage from Lake Michigan for
year at the North Point pumping station amounted
twenty-three and one-half billion gallons which was
average daily pumpage of over sixty-four million g
lons, an increase of two and one-half million gall
over the 1921 record. The maximum pumpage for a
one day was on September 6 when 91,857,980 gall
were pumped and the minimum on April 16 wh
43,743,000 gallons were pumped. The average
capita daily consumption was one hundred twenty-f
gallons. The maximum rate of pumpage or "peak"
the highest pumpage day was 107,000,000 gallons
twenty-four hours, while the maximum rate of c
sumption during this period was 119,000,000 gall
in twenty-four hours. In the "peak" hour the stage
water in the reservoir was lowered six inches. T
amount of water repumped at the High Service pun
ing station was 1,461,096,900 gallons. In addit
thereto four high service pumps located at the No
Point pumping station delivered 11,370,577,500 g
lons of water directly into the high level district. T
water delivered into the high level district was 54
per cent of the total pumpage.

The fire department pumped 22,471,800 gallons
water from the mains in fighting fires and in addit
used an equal amount of river water which was pump
into the high pressure fire mains which have no c
nection with the water department mains by the th
fire boats and fire engines.

It took 158,058,196 gallons of water which is sev
and one-half times the capacity of the reservoir,
sprinkle and keep the city streets clean. Of this,
street railway company used 32,198,300 gallons
sprinkle between its tracks. No charge is made
this water, but the company does the work.

It took 19,259 tons of coal to pump the water throu
the North Point pumping station and 997 tons more

arded. The work of excavating and concreting was
mmenced immediately. During the progress of the
cavation, the test boring data was found to be
ossly in error as quicksand was encountered over a
nsiderable area. It was then decided to pile the en-
e foundations with the exception of the east wall,
ich was to be carried on caissons according to the
iginal plans. Later piling was substituted for these
issons on account of the uncertainty of the
aring power of the subsoil and of the fact that
eir omission would greatly expedite the completion
the foundations. The work of piling proceeded con-
uously from the latter part of August and will be
mpleted early in 1923.

Plans and specifications for the superstructure are
ll under way. However, bids for furnishing and
ecting structural steel were let during the summer.
ds for three, four hundred horse power water tube
ilers were asked and contracts let in order to allow
e completion of plans for the boiler room floor. The
mping engines, contracted for in 1921, are com-
eted and ready for installation. However construc-
n of the plant was delayed by the extra time re-
ired for piling the foundations.

## burban use of water

Of the total pumpage 3,166,984,151 gallons, or 13.39
r cent, were delivered beyond the city limits. The
al revenue derived from the sale of water was $1,-
,833, of which $425,691, or 21.72 per cent, was paid
users living outside the city limits. The city of
rth Milwaukee used 187,144,700 gallons of water last
ar, while the villages of Shorewood and Whitefish
y combined, with a far greater population, used
ly 160,852,100 gallons. The difference was caused
the extensive use of water by North Milwaukee in-
stries. The city of West Allis, with larger in-
stries and also with a larger population, used 452,-
,400 gallons, while the county institutions west of
auwatosa used 391,706,100 gallons. The city of
auwatosa had its own water supply.

## stribution system

The distribution system was extended during the
ar by laying of over fifteen miles of water mains
d by the annexation of territory containing over
e mile of mains. The total length of the system with-
the city limits is now 537 miles.

The extension of the distribution system into dis-
cts, remote from the pumping station and located at
her levels and the impossibility of maintaining sat-
actory pressures at these points during the time of
h consumption due to the loss of head by friction
the present long lines of small diameter mains has
de it necessary to lay a fifty-four inch feeder main
Chambers street extending westward and connecting
with many of the cross mains. The work on this
in is being done in sections. The contract for the
t section was let in the latter part of 1921 and com-
ted early in 1922. At this time the question as to
ether it was advisable to continue laying cast iron
e, taking into consideration the lower price of steel

which eleven were due to electrolysis, occu
the year. The most serious of these occu
vember when the gate valve at the end of t
inch stub main in Chambers street, at the
Humboldt avenue, gave way after the co
removed the bulkhead and timber in orde
this main with the fifty-four inch feeder
Riverside pumping station grounds with
off the water or adopting some other meth
the thirty-six valves in place. The result
one-third of the west side without wate
thirds with a greatly reduced pressure.
the department was able to shut off the
valves and restore normal pressure w
hours. The property damage was very sli

## Water rates and collection system

The city charges a uniform rate of sev
hundred cubic feet, which is equal to ni
third cents per thousand gallons, for wate
within the city limits and ten cents per hu
feet, which is equal to thirteen and one
per thousand gallons to water furnished ou
city limits. In addition to charges for wate
a service charge of two dollars per annum
against every meter regardless of size or
or amount of water consumed. Unmetere
private fire protecting systems (automatic
pay twenty-five dollars per year for fou
nections and fifty dollars per year for si
nections. At the close of the year ther
four inch, 65 six inch and 1 eight inch, o
480 unmetered connections to automatic spr
ices.

There are 70,298 meters in use in the cit
eight per cent of all services are metered,
eight per cent of the departmental receipt
from metered services. A total of 17,825
repaired during the year of which 8,355 we
at the department shop and the remain
premises.

All meters are read monthly, but the la
are read every two weeks or oftener, and
meters for construction purposes are read

Water rates are collected quarterly.

## Water purification

The treatment of water supplied to th
continuous during the year. Bacterial test
and untreated water are made from sampl
three times daily. Copies of each analys
nished the superintendent of water works
the commissioner of health and to the sta
health monthly. The laboratory records
cate very wide and very sudden variati
bacterial count in both the raw and tre
Chlorine was applied in quantities varyin
teen to fifty-six ounces per million gallon
A bacterial reduction of over eighty-five per
ed from this treatment but the quality o
drinking water is still below the standard
United States public health service for drin

## POLITAN SEWERAGE COMMISSION
 of the county of Milwaukee

### ion and duty

erage commission was organized in 1913 un-
rity of a statute which provided that the
hould be selected by the mayor and hold of-
ts work was completed in every respect. Va-
e filled by the mayor in the same manner
l appointments. Funds were raised by a
ax upon all taxable property and by bonds
 and issued by the common council.

mission was charged with the duty of de-
d conducting a system for the collec-
mission and disposal of house and oth-
and drainage of the city. This involved the
f the proper method of disposal and of a
e and the bringing of the sewage to the
isposal. A site at the north end of Jones
he harbor entrance was finally selected and
 experimentation the activated sludge meth-
sal was adopted. Further extensive experi-
was carried on before the details of disposal
onstruction were decided upon. About thir-
 intercepting sewers have been constructed
e sewage of the city to the central plant.

the legislature created a metropolitan sew-
rict and commission to provide adequate
or the disposal of sewage from the entire
istrict of the three rivers within Milwau-
, which flow through the city of Milwaukee.
ing of the project was imposed upon prac-
entire Milwaukee county with the exception
 portion, which is not within the drainage
er the metropolitan act, the financing of
 be done by the Milwaukee sewerage com-
s imposed upon the drainage district of the
ll plans and specifications are subject to
val by the city sewerage commission.

### sludge

rated sludge process of sewerage disposal
 passing the raw sewage through aeration
e air is diffused through it and where it is
with millions of bacteria which act upon
tter. After being treated in these tanks
six hours, it is passed into sedimentation
 the sludge settles to the bottom, a portion
 returned to the raw sewage before enter-
ks to stimulate the purifying process and
 of which is dewatered and reduced to fer-

feet per minute to ten pounds pressure and three
tric generators each of 625 K. V. A. capacity; a I
house containing four boilers each having a cap
of 734 boiler horse power when operated at a no
capacity and 1,568 horse power when operated
two hundred per cent or a total maximum 6,272 I
power; complete coal and ash handling equipmen
sludge dewatering plant containing thirty Oliver fi
each eleven and one-half feet in diameter by foul
feet long and capable of producing a maximum of
four hundred tons of sludge cake containing eighty
cent moisture per twenty-four hours; and a sludge
ing plant which includes five hot air driers each s
feet long by eight-four inches in diameter capabl
producing one hundred and twenty tons of dried sl
per twenty-four hours.

### Cost and financing

The total cost of the sewage disposal system wi
in the neighborhood of $15,000,000 which is app
mately evenly divided between expenditures for
construction of the intercepting sewer system an
the disposal plant. The work has been carried on s
1914, and until 1921 the project was financed by
city through taxation and the issuance of bonds. S
1921 it has been financed by Milwaukee county. I
expected that the plant will be ready for opera
early in 1924. Annual cost of operation will be in
neighborhood of $800,000. This cost will be me
part by the sale of sludge. Experiments are b
conducted in conjunction with the federal departn
of agriculture to determine its value and mar
ability.

### Progress of the work in 1922

The grit house, valve houses and coarse screen ho
have been completed; the power and boiler plants
practically completed and the aeration and sedimer
tion tanks are nearly one-half completed. The
chinery for the power house is built ready for insta
tion and nearly all the boiler plant equipment is b
and ready for installation as soon as the house is ur
roof. Contracts have been let for the fine screens
for furnishing the five dryers.

Contracts have been let for building the disp
plant amounting to $4,766,920 of which $2,045,250
bracing sixteen special contracts were let in 1922.
present there are twenty-three separate contracts
der way in various stages of completion.

In addition to the work on the disposal plant,
commission has been engaged during the year exte
ing the intercepting sewerage system for which it
let six contracts amounting to $343,225 and embrac
the construction of approximately three miles of sew

### Metropolitan district

In 1921 the metropolitan sewerage commission fi
the boundaries of the metropolitan district, which
in the same drainage district as Milwaukee, so as
include practically the whole of Milwaukee county
cepting the city of South Milwaukee, the towns of (

Lake.

our contracts have been entered into, amounting
900,331.52, and embracing about six miles of sewers
n twenty-four to sixty-six inches in diameter. These
ers are being built for Shorewood and Whitefish
, for the city of North Milwaukee and town of
waukee; for the city of Wauwatosa and Town of
uwatosa. The commission is ready to award two
e sewers as soon as the rights-of-way are obtained.

## ter purification

he commission has reached the conclusion that with
completion of the disposal plant, its treatment and
continuance of chlorination will remove all danger
ewage pollution from the water supply. This con-
ion is based upon the fact that all sewage and a
ion of the storm water of the county will pass
ugh the plant where experiments indicate that
e than ninety-five per cent of the suspended organic
ter and bacteria will be removed. The commission
mates that raw sewage amounting to 26,353,000,000
ons per year is now discharged into the three riv-
flowing through the city though seventy-five out-
, and 4,340,000,000 gallons in addition are delivered
ctly into the lake through the old Menomonee inter-
ing sewer. It believes that the storm water over-
into the river and lake will not appreciably affect
water supply.

## BOARD OF HARBOR COMMISSIONERS

liam George Bruce, chairman
net Larson
I. Pinckley
d C. Reynolds
F. Ringer
man Bleyer, secretary

## anization and duties

he board of harbor commissioners consists of five
bers appointed by the mayor subject to confirma-
by the common council. The board has the power
nake all plans for the development of harbor fa-
ies including docks, wharves, warehouses and rail-
connections, to provide for and supervise the con-
ction, maintenance and repair of such facilities
has jurisdiction over all docks abutting public
s and the dock lines of the various channels of the
bor. All plans must be ratified by the common
cil before they can become effective.

## eral aid to local harbor project

rogress on Milwaukee's greater harbor project reed marked impetus during the year 1922. The act
Congress making provision for the improvement of
waukee harbor was approved on September 22, with
result that the war department appropriation bill
1923 includes an estimate of $618,000 for harbor
rovement and maintenance in Milwaukee. The work
engthening the present outer breakwater and the
truction of an additional arm to the same extend-
from a point on the south shore of Milwaukee bay
point opposite the harbor entrance will be inaug-
ed during the year. The cost of the completed
kwater is estimated at $4,592,000. Money will be

Company, which will give the city possessi
shore lands as far as Wilcox street.

While the commissioner of public works w
ering the matter of benefits and damages
tion with the condemnation of the propert
of the steel company solicited a conference
board of harbor commissioners for the purp
fecting a compromise which would be mutua
tageous. A suggestion by the officials of the
pany involves an exchange of its property
Wilcox street into the lake to make up for
of land on the north which the city is abo
over. Legislative sanction will be necessary,
permitting the exchange of property areas
submitted to the legislature for enactment.
promise, if effected, will permit harbor devel
continue uninterruptedly and will also enabl
nois Steel Company to enlarge its plant an
its lake terminal facilities.

## Grading of north harbor tract

Meanwhile attention is being given to the
of the harbor entrance, which is in bad shap
of indiscriminate dumping of earth and all
refuse for many years past. In some place
terial has been deposited to a height of fro
twelve feet. The entire area is being brou
to a level of five feet above city datum. It is
that about 125,000 cubic yards will have to l
by the contractor before the work is compl

## Street and dock construction

In addition to the work in connection with t
project, two street end docks, one at th
Prairie street and the other at the foot o
street were constructed. The new docks, i
to being provided with iron protecting rai
equipped with heavy timber bumpers extend
the dock and a little back of the fender rail a
ure of protection against automobile trucks.

## Commercial survey of tributary territory

A commercial survey of the areas of the
Northwest, tributary to Lake Michigan port
being prosecuted by Professor F. C. Blo
University of Wisconsin, under the auspic
board. The study, which will be very exh
being made with the purpose of determining
possible the trend and growth of the future
of the port and the character of terminals
have to be provided to accommodate the sam

## Menace of low water

The water level of Lake Michigan is st
creasing because of diversion of water into
tary drainage canal at Chicago. This is tr
the great lakes and their connecting wate
Michigan registers fully a foot below the te
erage during the closing months of the seaso
At present something like 10,000 cubic feet
per second are being taken from Lake Mic
year round. The permit under which Chic

# The
# Milwaukee Harbor
# Project

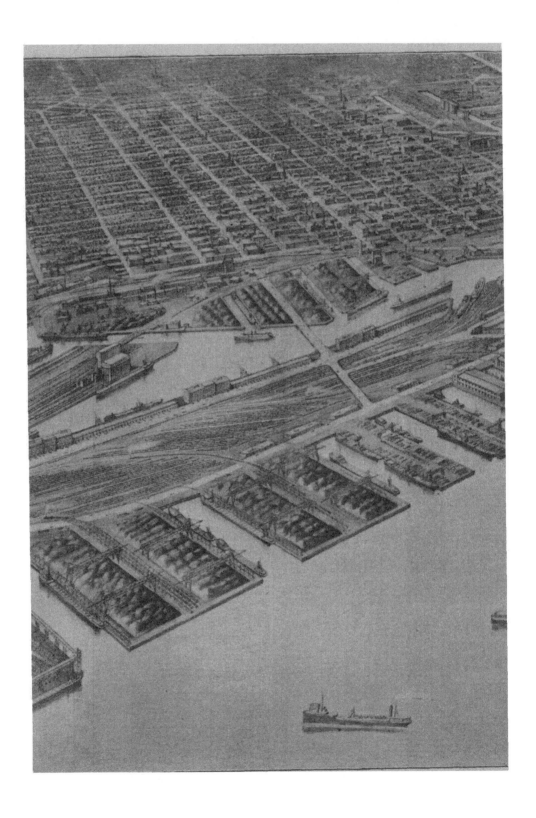

sformation of Jones Island 1914-23 from a Fisherman's Village to the Site of a Sewage Disposal Plant and Harbor Base.

I to bring suit in behalf of the state of Wisconsin
inst the state of Illinois and the sanitary district
Chicago, to check the unlawful obstruction of the
ters of Lake Michigan. An action was accordingly
un before the supreme court of the United States
ich is now pending.

t a conference of representatives of Wisconsin and
chigan ports held at Manitowoc, Wisconsin, March
nd 2, 1923, resolutions were adopted urging the
orney general of Wisconsin to press suit to an
ly conclusion. The Chicago sanitary district in
n invited the governors and attorneys general of
sconsin, Michigan, Minnesota and Indiana to a con-
ence at Chicago on Monday and Tuesday, March
and 20. Mr. William George Bruce, president of
board, attended the conference on invitation of
orney general Herman L. Elkern of Wisconsin.
e state of Michigan will join Wisconsin in prosecut-
the action against the sanitary district.

# REET RAILWAY AND ELECTRIC POWER ACQUISITION COMMITTEE

d S Hunt, chairman
lliam E. Black
J. Handley
e H. Olsen
n W. Radke
ul Gauer
n Koerner
n Doerfler, Jr.
n M. Niven

rtin G. Glaeser, secretary

## ganization and scope of work

The committee was appointed in 1919 by the presi-
it of the common council under authority of council
olution to investigate and report upon the advisa-
ity of purchasing the street railway, electric light-
and power property of the Milwaukee Electric
ilway and Light Company and various other ques-
ns of policy and fact connected therewith. Work
on this problem began shortly before the opening of
!0. Detailed reports upon corporate and financial
tory, service, valuation and public policy were pre-
ited to the council in July, 1921, but not printed. A
nmary report with recommendations as to a future
irse of action in franchise negotiations was printed
public distribution as a basis for its work, the
amittee was active in securing the passage of legis-
ion which would allow the negotiation of a franchise
h as it recommended.

## ntracts, negotiations and provisions

in the fall of 1921 the committee was authorized to
gotiate an operating agreement with the company
ich could be submitted to the council for its ap-
oval and which, in event of approval, should be sub-
tted to the electorate in a referendum election.
The committee's activities during the past year have
n entirely in the direction of reaching such an
reement and a draft of the same has been prepared,
only unfinished portion of which is the formula
der which the rate of return to the company upon

district surrounding the city, extending on
as far as Whitefish Bay, on the west to
and on the south to South Milwaukee. Her
braces within its terms the operation not c
urban and suburban railway inclusive of
and suburban operations by motor bus, e:
interurban service and also the operation of
light and power services and all heating serv
ed within the district. So far as operatic
the city are concerned, the adjustment of
control of service remains with the rail
mission of Wisconsin, but the city is given
to apply to the railroad commission for orc
ing into effect the provisions of the contr
outside district. Any customer, resident, in
who feels that he is unjustly discriminated
a result of any order issued by the city may
the railroad commission, but he must first ;
case to the city commissioner. This proce
to the city a large measure of "home rule"
local utilities, the railroad commission, functi
as a board of appeal and as a board of :
The value of the property is definitely fixed
tract, and the rules under which the valt
ascertained for any future date will likew
bodied in the agreement. These rules are bi
ly upon the investment theory of valuation.
value which furnishes the basis for computii
of return also serves as the basis for com
purchase price.

The agreement provides that the city
chase the property at any time upon six mo
to the company. The city may therefore cc
question of purchase at any time with a full
of what the purchase price will be. If the
cises its purchase option under the contract,
be no additional allowance for going value
there be reappraisal of the company's prc
additional allowance for severance damag
the property purchased is less than the entit
owned by the company. It is provided, how
the city must render the company such :
reasonable rates on behalf of the property
as it was customarily getting before the
chased the property.

The contract further provides that the
invest funds obtained from the sale of its
from other city sources, or derived to a lim
out of earnings, under a special type of
the company called the "municipal mortgage
also invest the money receiving credit the
city equity account. Upon money furnishe
pany for which the city gets securities undei
cipal mortgage, it will receive an intere
Upon money furnished the company for w
ceives credit in the city equity account it y
a return equal to the average rate of divi
on preferred stock. To the extent to whi
furnishes the company money for investn
the first of these arrangements, a substant
rate of return will be allowed the company.

Miscellaneous provisions give the city th
control the various operating and depreciatic
properly disposes of these reserves in the ev

books of the property accounts of the coming with the year 1914. The railroad com-
been of assistance in this connection.

these local utilities, at the same time safeguardi
the interests of the company.

# PROTECTION OF LIFE AND PROPERTY

## POLICE DEPARTMENT

ubenheimer, chief
enheimer, inspector
rory, captain
E. Bradley, police surgeon
onner, lieutenant, central station
dt, lieutenant, precinct number two.
ehlow, lieutenant, precinct number three
vski, lieutenant, precinct number four
eineman, lieutenant, precinct number five
nz, lieutenant, central station, night duty
nour, lieutenant, detective bureau
Pietersom, secretary
hek, superintendent of identification

## Organization

The police department consists of five police pr
cincts and the detective, traffic, identification and me
cal bureaus. The central police station is located
police headquarters, the others on the north, sou
and west sides and in the Bay View section of t
city. The precincts are in charge of lieutenants du
ing the day and sergeants acting as lieutenants
night except the central station which is in charge
a lieutenant at all times. The department maintai
five patrol wagons and two ambulances.

The department is better officered than it was pri
to 1921, but the various police precincts at night a
still commanded by sergeants with the rank of acti

he department is self undermanned. The increase
need of traffic men is constantly drawing men
m patrol duty with the result that a number of the
ts are too large for adequate covering.

wo policewomen were added during the past year
do work among women and children. They have
n assigned to work with the detective division of
ce force.

## me situation

Milwaukee's reputation as a relatively "free-from-
ne" city was maintained during the past year.
commission of major crimes has been on the de-
ase for several years. Crime waves are unknown.
murder rate is the lowest in cities of its size, and
same can be said of most of the other major
nes. Systematic burglaries, confidence games and
l-ups are not upon the city's crime calendar.

he number of complaints made to the police author-
s totaled 5,551, all of which were investigated by
detective bureau. This division made 3,262 ar-
s and cleared 2,272 cases.

he number of arrests totaled 16,899 of which 15,595
e of men and 1,304 of women. This is an increase
over one thousand in the number over the previous
r, but is more than accounted for by the increase
he number of violations of laws regulating vehicu-
traffic. Of the total number of arrests 5,314 were
state cases, 11,368 for city offenses and 217 for
cellaneous cases. About one thousand persons were
ested on suspicion. About one-half of the total
ests were for violations arising out of or in con-
tion with the use of motor vehicles.

f the persons arrested, 12,098 were natives of the
nty, 1,323 of Austria-Hungary, 813 of Germany,
of Russia, 673 of Poland, 286 of Greece, and 259 of
y. Between fifty and one hundred natives of Jugo-
via, Ireland, Sweden, Canada, Norway and Eng-
l were arrested.

he classification of persons arrested as to age
ws 1001 were under 17 years of age; 1,535 between
and 21; 6,024 between 21 and 30; 5,002 between
and 40; 2,717 between 40 and 50; 1,021 between 50
60 and 299 over 60.

he total number of arrested persons shows that
2 were married and 8,227 were single. White per-
s were arrested to the number of 16,412, black 473,
ow 11 and red 3.

## minal identification

hotographs, Bertillon measurements and finger
ts of 523 prisoners were made, necessitating the
ting up of 1,569 Bertillon cards and the taking of
2 sets of finger prints. In addition, 114 sets of
er prints and Bertillon records were taken of
soners who were "roughed." Through exchange with
national bureau at Washington, D. C., the bureau at
venworth, Kan., and the various police departments
he country, the records of 6,100 criminals and the
tographs, Bertillon measurements and finger prints
,167 thieves from other cities were obtained for the
of the department. These records are invaluable

work is accomplished by the close observatio
records. They tell what crimes are being
and where, what the department is doing a
complished and what there is for it to do.
tice of requiring detectives to write down
of each investigation tends to make them n
vant and eliminates the necessity of dupli
work at a latter date. Matters now being
filed and made accessible for future use are
records, photographs, finger prints, compla
rants, records of stolen automobiles, pawn
and lost goods, circulars describing persons
by police authorities in other cities, copies
checks and correspondence.

## Stolen property

The amount of property reported lost
totaled $687,851 and the value of property
$419,603. Of the stolen property $59,271 wa
lary, $18,633 by forgery, $100,213 by fraudu
of bank check, $34,692 by highway robbery
by automobile thefts, $110,999 by grand la
$32,437 by other forms of larceny. Of prope
at $48,104 reported stolen, the amount reco
valued at $24,556.

The installation of a stolen and recovere
room is one of the new phases of local po
Articles of all descriptions, valued at app
$34,000 and numbering 2,284, were handle
this room. Cash and bonds amounting to $3
turned over to the rightful owners.

## Automobile thefts

During 1922, 467 automobiles were stole
waukee of which 399 were recovered. Of
eries, 1009 were accounted for through the
71 automobile thieves. The value of a
stolen was approximately $350,000 and of th
ered $300,000. The average value of each
was $605. In addition 48 automobiles valued
were recovered for other cities. The recove
of-city cars is possible through the systema
which are maintained. Over 45,000 stolen a
from all parts of the country are described
in the department.

All purchases of used cars are reported
records searched for reports of thefts.

## Pawn shop accounting

Every article, reported, lost or stolen, no m
large or small, is listed by the department an
against the daily reports of goods pawned
the local pawn shops and second hand stores.
checking of these reports, the department w
recover property amounting to $7,859 and to
cases reported to it. A large number of ar
effected through this method of obtaining cl

## Forged checks

A facsimile copy of every worthless check
the city is kept as part of the permanent
the department. In addition a description o

ifferences, social conditions in the home and
rty are the chief reasons why adults leave
der girls return home less frequently than
they do not have retaining home ties and
y adjust themselves to new surroundings.
dren and older boys are practically always

years it had been the custom to pin circu-
sons wanted or missing on the bulletin board
dust and dirt made them impossible to be
reupon they would be thrown away. Now
ept on file so that they may be used.

letin

lication of the daily bulletin or look out for
anted by the police authorities was con-
he bulletin furnishes the uniformed patrol-
ll as the detectives, with descriptions of per-
ed and missing persons; of stolen automo-
cles and property; and of other data valu-
police officer. It is the means of encourag-
iformed officer to be on the lookout daily for
and stolen property. Many arrests, con-
nd    clearances
ints have re-
m its publica-
formed men are
rests of "want-
s which would
impossible pre-

me reports

ly crime report
e kinds of pos-
e and, under
hows the num-
ests, number of
ed and the val-
roperty stolen,
recovered. Not
it show the
e situation, but,
ulative feature,
he crime situa-
e portion of the
year up to the
ue.

of warrants

thod of hand-
inal warrants
systematized
e year. Pre-
re had been no
in this matter;
were scattered
he various pre-
me filed and
Under the new
,166 criminal
were filed and
A separate
ent is kept of

One hundred men are assigned to traffic w
Twenty-eight are motorcycle men while sixty-four
er thirty-six day and eight night posts. Patroll
are placed at the street crossings in front of forty-
schools to protect the children going to and f
school.

Over 6,400 violations of traffic laws were repo
during the year. Of these 2,694 were violations of
parking ordinance, 1,414 of speed ordinances, 639
obstruction of traffic, 5009 of the arterial high
stop law, 305 for reckless driving, 245 for viola
of laws requiring numbers on motor vehicles, 150
driving while intoxicated.

The mere mechanical work of protecting the pu
and informing it of the law is quite a task. For
stance, over seven miles of white lines, mostly to m
safety zones, must be painted on the pavements tv
each month. Safety zone posts and post bases have t
made, erected, kept in repair and painted three time
year. Five hundred "no parking", fire plug, sch
hospital and miscellaneous signs are made annu

## Vehicular accidents

The number of vehicular accidents for the y
totaled 3,375; 65 de
were caused by th
Thirty-eight of t
deaths were caused
automobiles and tr
striking pedestrians.
the accidents about 2
were the result of a
mobile, truck and m
cycle collisions.

The location of each
cident is marked o
large map on the wal
the traffic bureau offic
that is possible to tel
a glance just where
bulk of the accidents
occurring.

Each morning a re
is compiled showing
daily, monthly, and
nual record of accid
and of traffic violati
During the summer
1922 the daily record
something as follows:

Traffic accidents:
    Automobile colli
        ions _____
    Auto strikes child
    Truck-street c a
        collision _____
    Auto strikes sta
        tionary object__
    Auto-wagon colli
        ions _____

Traffic violations:
    Auto speeders

# DAILY BULLETIN

## MILWAUKEE POLICE DEPARTMENT

June 13, 1923.

### LOOKOUT

1—DESERTER, U. S. ARMY. John Grace, 21 yrs.
old, 5 ft. 7 in. tall, ruddy complexion, light brown
hair, blue eyes; home supposed to be on the north
side.

2—FORGERY. Frank Hathaway, 35 yrs. old, 5 ft.
3 in. tall, 200 lbs., stout built, dark complexion,
dark hair; wore a gray cap and a dark blue suit.
Passed a worthless check on a woman at 1147
Forest Home Ave.

### STOLEN AUTOMOBILE

3—FORD COUPE, 1923 model, black body and gear-
ing, Goodrich tires, motor No. 7689410.

### STOLEN BICYCLE

4—CROWN, dark red with white stripes, double
frame, black luggage carrier, long rubber grips,
flag on bell, Fisk tires, serial No. F-16038.

### MISSING

5—HERBERT HENTZ, 854 33rd St., 15 yrs. old,
5 ft. 7 in. tall, 135 lbs., well built, dark complexion, black hair, dark brown eyes; wore gray cap
and a brown suit.

6—FRANK KUHL, 1320 Cherry St., 15 yrs. old, 5
ft. 5 in. tall, 115 lbs., medium built, dark complexion, brown hair; wore gray cap, green sweat-
er, long khaki pants, khaki shirt, and white
shoes.

7—JOSEPH GRITZ, 331 29th Ave., 38 yrs. old, 5 ft.

he unifromed men in the department under the
of lieutenant were attending one class for one
each week. Instructions are given by lectures,
times illustrated by motion picture slides; prac-
training in putting on splints and bandages, per-
ing artificial respiration and carrying injured
ons is also given. Fifteen classes averaging 45
per class each are now being held. These classes
held in off duty hours. Special classes are held
men who miss instruction for any reason.

## plaints

tring 1922, 5,692 complaints were handled, filed
indexed. Under the system established at the
ming of the year, complaints are assigned to
tives for investigation immediately after they
made. Within twenty-four hours they are de-
ed to the bureau of identification where all infor-
on pertaining to pawned goods is listed for check-
against the reports of the pawn brokers and second
dealers. All information pertaining to automo-
is put on file with the automobile records and
in the day the greater part of the daily bulletin
mpiled from these complaints. The reports are
classified according to precincts, and a record
to each of them so that the officers in charge may
knowledge of what has occured in their precincts.

## ce alarm system

he police department maintains its private alarm
telephone system to keep in connection with the
bers of the force. Its duty is so quiet and so un-
sive that the general public scarcely knows how
a touch the department keeps with the individual
bers of the force. Over four hundred police alarm
s are scattered over the city, each connected with
central alarm station in the central police station.
patrolman, detective and sergeant calls at least
y hour. If a patrolman, fails to call within five
tes of his set time, his sergeant sets out to find
what is the trouble. If the patrolman is trailing
spect or in need of assistance, the failure to make
iourly call to the department may bring him just
elp he needs. On the other hand, if the depart-
wishes to give a general alarm, the flash on top of

answered by the department's five patrol wag
sons, numbering 12,553 were given rides, i
partment patrol wagons.

The police ambulance responded to 2,411
greater number of which were to transfer inj
sons to hospitals or to their homes.

## Delinquent personal property tax collect

All delinquent personal property taxes a
over to the police department after each tax
period for final collection. The total so turne
1922 amounted to approximately $525,000 of
department collected approximately $350,00
refusal to pay levy is made upon the proper
person owing the taxes. This work necessi
writing and distributing of 2,500 tax bills an
during the past year.

## Delivery of mail and notices

Few people know that the policemen upon
are carriers of the city's official mail and n
a policeman knocks at your door some day, he
be there to deliver an official notice from th
ment of public works. During 1922, 128,2
letters were delivered and 12,318 notices
this manner.

## Personnel

There were 743 men in the department at
of 1921 as against 591 at the close of 1920.
235 were assigned to the central, 89 to the s
121 to the west side, 96 to Bay View, 106 to
side stations and 96 to the traffic bureau. D
year there were 120 appointments. Twenty-
bers, including one detective and twenty
were retired on pension and three patrolmen
lieutenant died. Forty-three members of
were brought to trial for violating the rul
department. Of these thirty were fined, two
in rank, three reprimanded and eight dismis
the force. Four of these, however, appeal
board of fire and police commissioners and w
stated, nothwithstanding the adverse report
trial board.

Fire boats in Action

## FIRE DEPARTMENT

Clancy, chief engineer
Linkman, first assistant chief engineer
an Toor, assistant chief engineer
. Hanlon, assistant chief engineer
ith, assistant chief engineer
se, assistant chief engineer
Morgan, assistant chief engineer
son, assistant chief engineer
rphy, assistant chief engineer
hupe, assistant chief engineer
McCarthy, assistant chief engineer
inke, assistant chief engineer
ch, assistant chief engineer
Hanrahan, secretary

ion
epartment consists of forty-four companies,
wenty-eight engine companies, three fire-
anies, twelve truck companies, a rescue
e prevention bureau and a maintenance and
ice. The companies are located in various
e city so as to cover fire calls effectively.

on
artment is now seventy-five per cent mo-
he 1922 purchase of motor equipment con-
our combination pumpers and hose wagons
epartment twenty motorized pumping units
serve. This leaves eight engine companies
-drawn apparatus still in service. The de-
opes that sufficient funds will be set aside
these companies during the next two years
se-drawn equipment has outlived its useful-
not giving efficient service. Two second-
-Arrow chassis were purchased during the
ebuilt in the department shop, one for the

use of the rescue squad and the other a double ta
chemical engine. The price paid for the original to
ing cars, plus the cost of rebuilding them, is less th
fifty per cent of the price manufacturers are aski
for this type of apparatus. At the same time th
two pieces of equipment will compare favorably w
anything in the country.

### Fire boat service

The purchase by the city of the fire-boat "Torren
from the Duluth and Iron Range Railway Compa
gives Milwaukee a fleet of three high class steel h
fire-boats. The price, $65,000, paid for this boat r
resents an actual bargain to the city, considering
fact that the boat has seen very little service and
only about ten years old. It is doubtful if a boat
this type could be built and equipped today for f
times the amount paid by the city for it.

### School of instruction

Alterations are now being made by the departm
in one of the downtown engine houses, so that it n
be used as a school of instruction for the officers a
members of the department. Under this system
the members will be given practical instructions
their duties, especially in the handling of the differ
tools and appliances carried on the various apparat
These changes and alterations will be completed ea
in 1923 and will work out to a decided advantage o
the old system of drilling the men in their respect
districts. A uniform course of instruction will be gi
which is impossible under the present system on
count of the difference of methods of the officers ha
ling the training in the several districts.

### Firefighting and losses

The fire loss for the year will reach approximat
one and one-half million dollars, a decrease of one n

## LARGEST FIRES OF 1922 AND FIRE LOSSES

| Name | Location | Kind of Building | Date | | Loss |
|---|---|---|---|---|---|
| Western Fuel Co., | Canal St., | | Feb. 13. | | $220,892 |
| ., | First Ave., | Box Factory, | Sept. 20. | | 157,624 |
| ol, | Garfield Ave., | | Feb. 20. | | 93,030 |
| lothing Co., | East Water St., | | Dec. 20. | (Est.) | 76,000 |
| nitting Co., et al, | Twelfth St., | | Mar. 5. | | 64,784 |
| Coke and Gas Co., | Greenfield Ave., | | July 5. | | 56,695 |

10,164 miles, laid 724,100 feet of hose, raised 45,- feet of ladders and worked 3,865 hours. There e 2,087 actual fires during the year as compared 1,768 actual fires in 1921, and 2,011 in 1920.

## e prevention

uring 1922 greater attention was paid to fire pre- :ion work than during any previous year. Over e hundred thousand inspections were made which e practically evenly divided between places within outside of the fire limits. Over ten thousand de- s were found and ordered remedied.

ll school houses, both public and parochial, were n thorough inspections by two assistant chiefs, iled for this purpose and two inspectors of the ding inspection department. Detailed reports re- ling conditions and necessary changes were sent to authorities in charge of them.

uring fire prevention week short talks on fire pre- :ion were given in all the public and parochial ols by uniformed members of the force. In ad- n fifty-seven talks on the subject "What To Do 'ase of Fire" were delivered to groups at various itutions and manufacturing plants in the city, hav- a total attendance of 32,120 persons.

n essay contest on fire prevention promoted by the irtment was participated in by four hundred school dren.

he chief recommends, as in previous years, that the prevention bureau be established by ordinance and ed in charge of an assistant chief with full power rder changes where fire hazards exist. This is not ible under existing ordinances.

## e runs to places outside of the city limits

here were fifty-eight runs to fires outside of the limits during the year, of which thirty-two were res in the town of Wauwatosa, ten each in the vil- of Shorewood and the town of Greenfield, and each in the villages of Whitefish Bay and West waukee and the town of Lake. Several serious occurred in the towns of Lake and Milwaukee to ch the local department did not respond until the ment of the cost of the run was guaranteed by n officials because the authorities had failed to keep necessary guarantee deposits with city treasurer.

he cost of making these runs is charged to the ernmental unit where the fire occurred, but this covers the actual cost of the run without taking consideration the cost of repairing apparatus aged in the run or expenses involved in caring men injured.

ll the towns and villages bordering upon the city. :pt the town of Milwaukee, maintain such deposits. town of Lake requires that, in case of fire, its ials be first notified and that the call for aid from waukee come directly from one of them.

## ldings, grounds and shop

he department maintains thirty-four fire houses, thirty-four separate pipe lines, six, eight, ten twelve-inch mains, extending for a total distance 2.66 miles, with 251 hydrants and 279 fire cisterns

## Personnel

The men in the department numbered 694 of the year which is the total number allowe nance. There were twenty-four appointme force and twenty-five promotions. There deaths in the department, four due to natu one from gun shot, one from falling from a three men from poisonous gas in a sewer National avenue.

Ten men, nine widows and fourteen chil placed on the pension roll. Over one hundre dollars was paid in pensions.

## FIRE AND POLICE ALARM SYS

Oscar D. Kleinsteuber, superintendent
Hugo A. Kleinsteuber, assistant superinten

The fire and police alarm system has cha maintenance of the city's private signalli used by the fire and police departments. T is really a double one. The street alarm c boxes in many cases contain compartments police and fire department telephones, but t partments are entirely shut off from each o arate switchboards are located in the police ters and in the central fire alarm station i hall.

During 1922 the capacity of the generatin the alarm system located in the city hall was doubled in the replacement of old equipme seventy-five volt one hundred ampere generat by a fifteen horsepower motor. The current is stored in storage batteries which operat ferent types of alarm service used by the fire departments and the signal lights upon als As the storage battery system is in continu one set has to be stored with electrical en the parallel set is discharging its energy.

Fire engine houses seven, nine and ten, wer with fire proof apparatus stands and the nec proof terminal boxes and conduit system. T new fire alarm and two new police alarm sta placed in service and combination fire and p posts were permanently established. The tot of fire and police alarm posts were permaner lished. The total number of fire alarm static 882, and total number of police alarm statio

The underground conduit system was exte ing the year by the laying of 2,197 lineal d vitrified clay conduit which is less than ter of the average yearly work of this nature. T of cable installed was less than one mile, b demands indicate that this class of work will extended within the near future. The aeria service was extended seventeen miles, whil one-half miles of aerial line were removed, gain of six and one-half miles in the aerial s

## BUREAU OF BUILDING AND ELEV INSPECTION

William D. Harper, inspector of buildings
William Gaethke, deputy inspector and e

in this bureau. Control is exercised through
ment that an occupancy permit must be
howing that the building conforms to the
nance.

## perations

operations for 1922 were valued at $31,287,-
is six million dollars in excess of building
for 1921, the greatest previous year. Of
t approximately $25,000,000 was for build-
tion and $1,200,000 for plastering. Permits
for the construction of 5,300 buildings and
on of 2,100. Concrete construction in new
mounted to $5,000,000, masonry construction
0; steel construction to $150,000 and wood
to $11,000,000. Of the concrete construc-
,000 was divided equally between factories
s; masonry construction was spread pretty
l classes of buildings; steel construction was
ined to small garages; and over $10,000,000
l construction was about equally divided be-
ex flats and dwellings. Over two hundred
mostly of wood construction, were razed to
for new buildings.

ease of building is not caused by large op-
any one line of work, but is quite general.
ry of industry from the depression is re-
n increase of $2,500,000 in factory and shop
n over 1921. Increases of $1,600,000 in du-
1,300,000 in theater, $250,000 in warehouse,
1 stores, $400,000 in dwellings, $350,000 in
store and flat dwellings, and $250,000 in
construction show how general the increase
only substantial decreases were of $1,000,-
ool and $400,000 in office building con-

000 permits were issued, and 85,000 inspec-
made of work under construction. The cost
ning the service was $85,000 while the reve-
$125,000, leaving a balance of $40,000 to be
r to the general city fund for overhead

g to figures, recently compiled, Milwaukee
elfth among cities of the United States in
perations, as compared to a population rank
. Last year, with a total of seven million
s than this year, Milwaukee ranked eighth
nited States cities. Considering the small
is city this is indeed a good showing.

uilding has been greater during the past year
ny year since 1912. A total of 2,960 homes
d, divided among 491 in 25 apartment build-
in 78 stores, 1,232 in duplex flats and 1,129
amily dwellings. The marked increase is in
r of duplex flats and single family dwellings.
the building of home apartments is con-
an even greater rate in 1923. The increase
uarters was about twenty per cent above the
nt to take care of the normal growth of the
there is still a shortage of seven thousand
the proper housing of the people of this city.

any encumbrance. The total mortgage debt upon
balance is estimated at $120,000,000. According to
1918 house count of the board of public land comm
sioners there were 38,950 one-family, 21,203 two-f
ily and 864 multiple family residences, 7,800 busin
and 2,137 factory buildings in the city.

Health department figures for 1920 record 2,
basement dwellings, 3,500 tenement houses, 500 ap
ments and 1,600 rooming houses.

A survey of greater Milwaukee by the Wiscor
Telephone Company in 1922 estimates a population
775,000 in 1942. The survey covers an area of
hundred seventy square miles, including all the s
urbs of the city of Milwaukee, excepting South 1
waukee. It revealed 123,426 families living in this
trict. Of these 48,071 families or 38.9 per cent liv
one-family homes, 67,426 families or 54.7 per cent
in duplex flats, 4,589 families or 3.7 per cent in ap
ments, 1,451 families or 1.2 per cent live in lodg
houses and 1,889 families or 1.5 per cent live in el
housekeeping apartments. An estimate of the gro
of the district calculates that in twenty years 39.3
cent of the families will live in one-family dwelli
51.6 per cent in duplex flats, 6.6 per cent in apartme
1.1 per cent in lodging houses and 1.4 per cent in l
housekeeping apartments. The large increase in
percentage of apartment house dwellers is based u
the increase in the number of apartment houses
recent years and the growing density and conges
of the population. Within the present city limits th
are 5,920 families to the square mile; outside the
limits there 220 families to the square mile and in
entire district 820 families to the square mile.

## Theater inspection

The electrical apparatus of 806 road shows and
deville acts was inspected during the past year.
these 743 were found to comply with the electr
code; 52 were ordered to fireproof their scenery
property, and 11 had their scenery removed from
theater for failure to comply with the city requ
ments. Changes were ordered on 165 electric eff
and in eight cases the effects were in such condi
that their use was not permitted.

The number of theaters and motion picture ho
now number eighty-two. One new picture house
opened during the year and two rebuilt and enlar
Late in December a permit was issued for the const
tion of a one million dollar theater on Grand Ave
which is now being built.

## School inspection

A joint inspection of all public and parochial sch
was made by the inspection bureau of the fire dep
ment and this department during the early par
1922 and a report of the condition of each schoo
gether with the recommendations for correction of
safe conditions was forwarded to the school b
and the pastor of each parochial school.

## Electrical maintenance men and contractors

Three examinations were held to allow person
qualify as electrical maintenance men and cont

am F. Steinel, sealer
rt Lueck, deputy

### es

e bureau of weights and measures is charged with
onduct of the city's public markets and with the
ction and testing of weights, scales and measures
ery kind to ascertain their correctness.

### kets

e eight public markets had a banner year in at-
ince and in the volume of business transacted.
rds show that 57,926 loads of produce were
ght to the markets as compared with 33,947 loads
921. Attendance also showed a large increase over
previous year.

nditions at several markets are such that it will
re more space to accommodate the large increase
isiness. The market at Mitchell street and Ninth
ue is the most overcrowded as there is only room
forty loads on the grounds and more than one
red were found to occupy the adjoining streets
any occasions. One account of the great increase
e value of property in this vicinity, the property
ig tripled in value in the past six years, the
r believes that it would be advisable to abandon
d look for a larger and less expensive site.

elter sheds were erected at the North avenue and
rell avenue market as a protection to gardeners
farmers having produce there. The rented stalls
crowded beyond their capacity on numerous occa-

### hts and measures

pectors of the department visited 8,400 places of
ess to check up the accuracy of weights and
ures in use. Out of a total of 53,470 scales,
its and measures tested during the year, 52,155
.5 per cent, were found to be correct. Fourteen
ors of the city ordinance were taken into court,
onvictions were obtained in each case.

ch time was spent during the year in checking
isoline measuring devices, and a number of pumps
could be manipulated to defraud the consumer
condemned and put out of use.

## )ARD OF EXAMINERS OF ENGINEERS

lard Kunz, chief examiner

### es and work

e board of examiners of engineers have charge of
xamination and granting of licenses to engineers,
en and operators of stationary and portable power
s, steam boilers and engines or appliances con-
d therewith. All licenses are graded as unre-
ed or restricted and of first, second or third class.
iinations are held daily at the convenience of the
:ants. Where the applicant is unable to write,
al examination is given.

ring the past year 2,485 licenses were renewed,

Charles Poethke, chief smoke inspector

### Duty

The bureau of smoke suppression has as
tion the enforcement of the smoke ordinan
makes the emission of dense smoke for any
ceeding five minutes in any hour of the day
an offense punishable by a fine or impriso
both. Both the Chicago and Northwestern
Chicago, Milwaukee and St. Paul railway:
inspectors who are responsible to the city bu

### Work

During the year 6,417 observations were
smoking chimneys and 114 complaints inv
Violations of the city ordinance were disco
nineteen instances. Of the complaints sixty-
of low pressure and heating plants and fif
power plants. The large number of complaint
emission of smoke from low pressure and
plants was due to the fuel shortage and div
smokeless coal to eastern centers by orders
federal government.

Forty-seven plants, providing for smokele
tion were installed during the year, and twe
under construction at its close.

Ninety-four engine crews of the Chicago, M
and St. Paul railway were reprimanded or t
of service for violations of the ordinance.

The placing of this department in the offi
bureau of building and elevator inspection
satisfactory as it has enabled this departme
amine plans for power and heating plants
that chimneys, breechings and boiler room c
to the requirements of the smoke ordinance b
building permit was granted.

### Recommendations

The department recommends that a perm
quired for the installation of low pressure and
plants so as to insure the installation of pl.
viding for smokeless operation, wherever w.
and that a fee be charged for the examir
plants and the granting of permits so that th
ment will be made self sustaining. At presen
are issued without charge.

## SAFETY COMMISSION

Dr. H. E. Bradley, chairman
Claude R. Diegle, secretary

### Organization and duties

The safety commission was created as an
body to the mayor and city officials and be
official body in 1921. Its duties are to investi
vise and report to the mayor, city council a
city officials as to the best methods of provi
the safety needs. The commission keeps a r
the accidental deaths occurring in the city.

### Educational work

# PUBLIC HEALTH

## HEALTH DEPARTMENT

Ruhland, M. D., commissioner of health
ompson, M. D., deputy commissioner
  Adams, vital statistics
  Barth, M. D., school hygiene
V. Bauer, M. D., communicable disease
  E. Church, bacteriology
  Cunliffe, chemistry
  Ernst, M. D., tuberculosis
Martin, R. N., nursing
  McKillop, M. D., venereal disease
ilgrim, M. D. C., food hygiene
hiller, M. D., South View hospital
  Thompson, M. D., sanitation

### tion

lth department has charge of all the city
in the field of public health and sanitation.
ad of the department is the commissioner of
whom is vested a wide range of duties and
he work of the department is divided among
us and divisions of child hygiene, school
uberculosis, field nursing, contagious dis-
ereal diseases, sanitation, food inspection,
stics and the chemical and bacteriological
s.

its quarters on the sixth and eighth floors
hall, which are entirely inadequate, the de-
maintains a station on the south side at
reet and Sixth avenue, and one on the north
20 North avenue and operates the South
agious disease hospital. The south side sta-
e moved to new quarters at Mitchell street
h avenue in a building now under construc-
new quarters will contain fifty per cent
which will allow a more efficient handling
Fifteen child welfare clinics are maintained
  and other public buildings. During the
ason, first aid stations under the joint con-
e department of health and public works
lished at the city beaches on account of the
er of accidents occurring there.

### lth conditions, 1922

conditions in the city of Milwaukee have
ained on the same high level as that of last
 general death rate per thousand popula-
compared with 9.6 last year, which was the
he history of the city and the lowest for any
  United States with a population over 300,-
s. The average age of death for all age
 1922 is 42.5 as compared with 39.8 for
ing the age period over five years, we find
 increase in the average length of life from
1 to 52.8 in 1922.

the diseases responsible for the greatest
  deaths, excluding deaths occurring in in-
records show those affecting the circulatory

births. It may be noted that the birth rate was
lowest for 1922 since 1900 when the first calculat
of this rate were made. In these years the birth
has been below twenty-four births per thousand p
lation in only three years, while, in the years
1910 to 1918 it was over twenty-six per thousand
year.

## CHILD WELFARE

### Child welfare

Sixteen child welfare clinics are held each wee
various parts of the city. These clinics are mainta
for well babies with the purpose of advising par
regarding their children so as to insure, as fa
possible, a normal, gradual and continuous growth
a happy childhood. The average attendance at
clinic was fourteen per day. A total of 10,668
were made for advice and 7,768 supposedly well ba
were brought for examination and measurement. N
instruction was given on the subject of milk form
and modification. In each case where informatio
this nature was requested, a nurse made a follow
visit the next morning to give any assistance or
ditional instruction that might be necessary.

### Nutrition classes

Nutrition classes were maintained in forty-
schools. In these schools, out of fifty-nine thous
children who were weighed and measured, seven t
sand were found to be more than ten per cent un
weight for their age and height. Nearly all ent
nutrition classes at the beginning of the year and
furnished a graham cracker and half a pint of
per day at a weekly cost to them of twelve ce
Children found to be more than ten per cent un
weight are given a physical examination as early
the school year as possible, and are referred for
correction of such physical defects as may be foun

### Routine work

The regular routine child welfare work of examir
children for day nurseries and the inspection of
ternity homes and baby boarding homes for licens
was continued without material change.

### Infant mortality

A study of the infant death rate, in so far as the
period from thirty days to one year is concerned, sh
a decrease from eighty-four per thousand births
1912 to thirty-six per thousand births in 1922.
death rate under thirty days, however, is the same
ten years ago, the intervening years being no be
and usually worse. This seemingly indicates the
of greater instruction and care in prenatal work wl
the department is, at present, unable to furnish.

An effort is made by the nurses to call upon moth
within two weeks after birth of every live baby and
give them the department book of instructions
infant care. In an effort to learn if additional c
might be of service to the mother in bringing the cl
safely past the first thirty days of life

ol enrollment totals 27,000. There are 148 schools
ll under inspection. For the purpose of this work
city is divided into twenty-two districts, each un-
charge of a physician. The schools in the dis-
t are visited by doctors and nurses on alternate
s on regular schedule. Frequently they meet at
'erences for the discussion of school cases or in
it of an imminent epidemic. The work of the
ol physician includes morning inspection, physical
minations and the supervision of sanitation of build-
s and grounds. On arriving at the school each
her is notified, and those children who seem to be
ng from any cause or who have been absent three
s continuously are sent to the physician. This
ctice works out as a splendid preventive measure
inst the spread of contagious disease as the chil-
n who show symptoms of on-coming sickness or in-
plete recovery are promptly sent home. It was also
sible to reduce the number of nurses' contagious
ase calls by over 6,700 by this practice. Wherever
ol sessions are interrupted for one week or more,
the children of the school are inspected class by
s to discover disease and prevent its spread. This
k has the increasing support and co-operation of
school teachers.

## amination work and results

t is the aim of the department to give all children
the schools physical examinations at regular in-
rals as far as possible. These are undertaken in
kindergarten, first, third, fifth and eighth grades.
ers are given in connection with special school
minations and at the time of application for work-
permits. These records are kept in the school the
ld is in. These cards should follow the child up as
moves from one school to another, to the continua-
a school, higher educational institutions or into the
ustrial world. These early histories are extremely
uable in later treatments of disease.

During the past year 58,000 children were handled
the school physicians at morning inspection, 45,000
the public and 13,000 in the parochial schools. Of
se 2,600 were excluded by the physicians and 7,000
the nurses. Approximately 45,000 examinations
re made, over 16,000 defects found, over 12,000 cor-
tions recommended and over 11,000 corrections se-
ed through the assistance of the nursing division.
nong the defects were 3,600 cases of diseased tonsils,
of adenoids, 8,832 of defective teeth, 2,631 of de-
tive vision, 37 of defective hearing, 47 of orthopedic
'ects, 81 of pulmonary disease, 130 of cardiac dis-
e and 81 of nervous disease, excluding mentally
l 826 of miscellaneous ailments. Besides these, 222
iminations were made and 75 defects discovered at
continuation schools.

The specialists connected with this division made
93 eye, 237 nose and throat and 93 ear examinations;
ated 431 eye, 11 nose and throat, and 17 ear cases.
erations were performed in 68 cases. The three
ntal clinics, maintained for the benefit of indigent
ool children admitted 5,729 patients for 8,132 sit-
gs.

Unreserved working permits were granted to 1,102
ldren, provisional permits to 3,197, provisional per-

## Need of psychiatric clinic

The department feels that the lack of adeq
ice to examine into the mental soundness of
is one of the greatest shortcomings in the
giene work. According to a survey in so
Milwaukee schools by Dr. Smiley Blanton, o
versity of Wisconsin and the National Com
Mental Hygiene, approximately seven pe
the children in the grade schools are in a
subnormal group. This is the group from
work of the juvenile court largely develop
criminal courts are supplied with material.
that an adequately officered psychiatric servi
ed to separate these unfortunates and refer t
proper environmental and institutional c
they can be trained to a life of usefulness
from a place where they may become a
society. Until the department is supplied
to develop this service, there is a splendid o
for private charity to undertake the respon
this work.

## FIELD NURSING

### Organization of work

A staff of sixty field nurses has been fairl
maintained during the year. Twenty-four
a supervisor operate from the south side s
eighteen nurses and a supervisor from bot
hall and the north side stations. The nurs
is organized on the generalized plan. Three
as relief and assistants to the supervisor
divides her time between work in conne
tuberculosis and emergency contagion work
nurses who specialized in child welfare
transferred to generalized work because i
apparent that greater good was being ac
than in the districts.

### Supervision

Adequate supervision for instruction is
important in so diversified a service as nur
the generalized plan to insure the work
balanced and economically planned. The
of a proper distribution and correlation
through the application of the generalized f
ice as compared with the individual serv
shown by a thirty-six per cent saving of
by overlapping calls. The saving in 1921 a
only twenty-one per cent.

The interest and efficiency of the nurse
greatly stimulated by lecture courses condu
department at which talks were given by
various health activities. Intensive course
en in both child welfare and contagious di

### Nursing education

Since the civil service requirements for a
to positions in the nursing division do not
special training or experience in public heal
it is necessary for the division to give its
preventive view-point to enable them

nutritional cases are accepted. The latter
eferred to the family physician or to the
pital.

ruction

icts are still so large that it is impossible
e some needed work such as group instruc-
is both popular and valuable in teaching
personal and household hygiene and child
hrough the summer, however, 565 girls
struction in little mothers' clubs. The
f the full time of one nurse was devoted
g classes in "Home Hygiene and Care of
ith a total attendance of 4,103. Frequent
were given to groups of girls, parents and
uring the summer visits were made to
unds where the director brought to the
ntion matters along health lines. A num-
aid classes were also conducted.

g on of new health activities is constantly
ands for extra nursing service, which has,
de necessary some decrease in older serv-
as tuberculosis and child welfare work.
e added during the past year were the in-
f the Schick test and the administration of
xin in the schools for diphtheria prevention,
f reported tuberculosis cases to see whether
till under physician's care and to check up
ses, the goitre survey at the opening of
he fall, the survey of crippled children
g and the follow up work incurred through
n from schools on suspicion during the
lemic.

work

ds for the year show that 11,636 calls were
public and 6,654 upon parochial schools. A
,270 school inspections and 107,925 home
ade. Of the home calls 58,578 were in con-
h physical defects, 37,548 child welfare,
school absentees, 11,025 with tuberculosis,
irth registry, 6,429 with suspected contag-
1,029 with boarding homes. An interest-
f school inspection work were the prelimin-
on to prevent children suffering from light
contagious disease from being admitted to
where they might infect other children.

OMMUNICABLE DISEASES

the year

tment's records show that the city was fair-
communicable disease, measles and whoop-
xcepted. The records show a total of six-
nd cases as compared with nine thousand
nd seventeen thousand for 1920. The in-
he total number of cases over the 1920
ccounted for by the fact that there were
hree hundred more cases of measles and
hundred cases of whooping cough. Ap-
nine hundred deaths were primarily due
us disease, but fifty-five per cent of the

take the necessary precautions of keeping the ch
dren isolated from well children. Their control, fro
a public health standpoint, is made difficult becau
they occur largely in a pre-school age period whe
they cannot be brought under the immediate suspe
sion and control of the health authorities.

Scarlet fever began to appear in a large number
cases toward the end of the year, but it was of
rather light variety and did not reach the epidem
stage until early in 1923.

Small pox

Small pox was held well in check in Milwaukee.
is especially gratifying to note that, while this disea
recurred with marked virulence in various distric
of the county where vaccination has been neglecte
there have been only one hundred and twelve cas
and two deaths in this city. This is largely due
the wide spread of vaccination of the children in t
public and parochial schools within past years,
that only children entering the lower grades or comir
to the city are of the non-immune type. Industry
beginning to appreciate the value of protecting itse
against disease. Compulsory and voluntary vaccin
tions were carried out in several industrial plant
and one firm now requires successful vaccination
all new employes. Approximately sixty-five hundr
vaccinations were made during the year of which ov
three thousand were school and twenty-three hundr
industrial vaccinations.

Diphtheria prevention

In line with the disease prevention activities of t
department has been the application of the Schick te
and the immunization of children against diphtheria
the use of toxin-antitoxin if found susceptible. Th
work was not started until fall. The service was o
fered to the parents of eight thousand children. O
of this number more than three thousand consen
were received that the test be performed and the ch
dren protected if found susceptible. Of this numb
more than seventeen hundred were found to be su
ceptible and more than twelve hundred have bee
immunized. Universal adoption of this test and in
munization against diphtheria undoubtedly will go
great ways toward wiping out, or at least reducin
greatly, diphtheria in Milwaukee. It may be noted th
the number of cases of diphtheria in the city has be
reduced from more than fourteen hundred in 1921
less than half this number in 1922.

Other protective measures

Among other protective measures directed immed
ately against development of contagious diseases, h
been the health supervision of those employed whe
food is handled and prepared. A special survey
dairy plants, groceries, restaurants was made in cour
of which more than thirteen hundred individuals we
examined. Seventeen exclusions were made becau
of the finding of contagious disease carriers amo
them. When it is appreciated that about eight p
cent of contagious diseases are conveyed by means
the hand to mouth, it will be understood what vit

...ied in the bacteriological laboratory during 1922. ...s is ten thousand examinations less than were ...ormed in 1921, which is accounted for by a de- ...se of sixteen hundred in the number of diphtheria ...minations on account of the comparative small- ... of this disease during the year. The number of ...erman, milk, ice and water examinations showed ...ncrease.

## TUBERCULOSIS

### ...erculosis prevention

...uberculosis has come to be regarded as a disease ...hildhood and as probably having the most danger- ...period in the first three or four years of life. Hence ...ideal method of prevention would be to care for ...children before the symptoms and signs of the ...ase become manifest. As tests have not yet been ...ciently perfected to detect slight deviations from ...nal, the division has to satisfy itself in detecting ...nany of the early forms as possible. The plan was ...liscover such children as appeared to be good soil ...the tubercle bacillus and then attempt to build up ...r vitality to withstand the infection of the germ ...ch is impossible for them to evade. With this in ...v a start was made on the examination of the chil- ...n in the schools. Fifty-four of the one hundred ...nty-nine schools in the city were visited and 941 ...s examined.

### ...ercular meningitis survey

...survey of forty-five cases of tubercular meningitis, ...overed in Milwaukee in the past two years revealed ...fact that, in sixty-five per cent of the cases, this ...ase occurred in families in which no source of in- ...ion could be found. It was also found that a com- ...atively long period of exposure occurred before an ...e form of tuberculosis actually occurred.

### ...pensary work

...he division dispensary work has been developed to ...extent that tuberculosis suspects have the oppor- ...ty of receiving careful physical examinations. In ...tal of 6,926 visits made for the purpose of con- ...ing the physicians at the city hall, south side sta- ...and north side station, there were 2,631 new pa- ...ts examined and 204 positive cases diagnosed. Dur- ...the year 485 new cases of tuberculosis were re- ...ed by physicians. There were 358 deaths in the ...ity institutions and in the city of which 61 were ...other than pulmonary tuberculosis.

...linics have been conducted every Thursday evening ...he city hall and south side station for persons that ...employed during the day.

### ...sh air schools

...uring the past year four fresh air schools for ...ol children suffering from some form of tuber- ...sis and diseased conditions which might easily lead ...uberculosis were in operation. They were attended ...289 children distributed as follows: Lapham park, ...; Third street, 51; Second avenue, 48, and Lincoln

proportion. It included 4,296 visits to the ...cluding examinations, consultations and ... of which 654 were by women. The number ...ual cases totaled 1,286, of which 271 we... Sixty-three new cases of syphilis and one hun... one new cases of gonorrhea were discovere... man tests were made in 1,758 cases, of ... showed a positive reaction.

## CHEMICAL LABORATORY

### Special chemical investigations

Fifteen special investigations, surveys and ...es were inaugurated or completed during 1... dition to the regular analytical, court, rout... and report work of the laboratory. Thre... dealt with the city water supply, namely: investigations of the bacterial efficiency of ... relation to the disinfection of lake water, ... bearing upon filtration and of the recurre... chlorophenolic taste in the city's drinking w... were sanitary surveys of the lake bathing b... of the upper Milwaukee river. Four dealing ... products covered the questions of the us... starch in powdered sugar to prevent lun... bulk and package oysters, of the quality o... extracts and of the bleached flour situation ... volved the increased amount of sulphur i... supply and the comparative amounts of ... gas supply at the gas works and the city h... miscellaneous investigations had to do wit... tion of types of rapid drying stove polish, ne... for the determination of the quantity of ... carbonated beverages, the alleged use of ars... coloring of Christmas tree ornaments and ... lead in stoppers of food containers.

### Milk Supply

The adoption of the weight and test meth... ing milk producers by city distributors h... the yearly decline in the average butter fat ... milk. This factor, together with the ado... more logical procedure in handling milk a... the plants, makes it possible to take a singl... sample of an entire shipment. The average ... content of all producers' samples was 3.6... and of retail dealers' samples 3.64 per cent. sample collected from retail dealers was ... legal standard of three per cent butter ... per cent of the samples collected from restau... below the legal standard, as compared to ... cent in 1921. The average per cent of n... cream sold by city dealers, as indicated by ... data on 568 samples was 23.38 per cent.

### Gas

A daily analysis of gas sold for illumin... poses shows that in two months, August a... ber, the average heating value fell very sli... than one-fifth of one per cent below the mi... quired by the state railroad commission, ... the majority of months the average was o... per cent above the requirement.

the laboratory do not seem to be able to
:cessfully eliminate these recurrences. In-
is being carried on with a view of still
roving conditions.

## content of beverages and prohibition
:ement

e passage of the city ordinance providing
ensing of places selling non-intoxicating
lyses were made of the alcoholic content of
beverages in order to determine which
t and which types might not be sold.

f 463 samples of alcoholic beverages were
during the year, representing an increase
cent over 1922.

pearances in court were made in furnishing
stimony in thirty-seven cases for the city,
state authorities.

## sh

eginning of the year the manufacturers of
g and inflammable stove polishes lodged
that the provisions of the regulatory ordi
e too rigid and could not be complied with.
stigation a number of types of efficient pol-
produced which fully met the requirements
and the code.

## flour

stigation of the bleached flour situation was
onjunction with the state dairy and food
er and of the claims of certain manufactur-
their product is matured or aged flour.
f baking tests, with freshly milled flour,
e and after bleaching, demonstrated the
these claims.

, all attempts to stop the sale of this product
state statute were nullified by an opinion by
ey general of Wisconsin, that interference
le of bleached flour in the original container
terference with interstate commerce and,
within the jurisdiction of state authority.

## rk

the year ninety-two appearances were made
rts to furnish chemical testimony in connec-
eighty cases. This is a decrease in the num-
pearances as compared with the preceding
a still greater number of cases the findings
oratory were accepted without a personal
e. It is expected that the number of per-
arances in cases will be still further dimin-
ng 1923 as the result of a policy providing
ceptance of the chemist's findings, without
timony, except in contested cases or cases
osition is anticipated.

## f analytical work

ume of analytical work decreased somewhat
of the previous year as a result of a partial
the character of samples handled and the

Over 45,000 inspections of food establishments,
increase of 10,000 inspections over 1921, were m
during the year, including 8,800 of meat markets,
000 of groceries, 7,800 of commission houses, 600
railway depots, 2,000 of bakeries, 5,700 of restaura
hotels and saloons. There were 152,000 post mort
of animals, including 17,400 of cattle, 124,000 of cal
13,000 of hogs and 9,000 of sheep. Of these 524
cases weighing 54,000 pounds were condemned. Th
were also condemned 42,000 pounds of dressed meat
meat markets and slaughter houses, 8,600 of poul
42,000 of candy, fruits, vegetables and cereals.

## Examination of food handlers

No person who has any contagious, infectious
venereal disease is permitted to work in any p
where food and drink is prepared, handled or off
for sale. Suspects are ordered to report to the he
department for examination. Several proprietors
quire their help to be examined at intervals to pro
the public against disease. This is a very good m
which should be encouraged. Every food han
should be examined every six months and licenses
quired as a means of control.

## Milk supply

The Milwaukee milk supply comes from four t
sand farmer shippers. In the past the health dep
ment has been responsible for seeing that the
product was clean. During 1922 the dealers, th
selves, put men into the field to see that the m
they secure, comes from healthy cattle and clean
roundings, and that it is produced and shipped in
proper manner.

At present ninety-eight per cent of all milk
in the city is pasteurized. All firms in this city
now using the holding system of pasteurization.

During the year 849 farms, of which 42 were bar
1,892 city milk plants, 228 county creameries, 368
milk cans, of which 1,480 were condemned as unfi
ship milk in, were inspected. A total of 5,229 can
milk were returned as unfit for human consump

## Licenses and prosecutions

The bureau issued 2,845 meat, 2,528 milk stores,
milk wagon, 497 peddler and 10 spring water licer
Fees collected and turned over to the city treas
amounted to $6,500.

A total of 103 violations of state and city he
laws, 34 cases of adulterated or unsanitary milk
69 miscellaneous cases were presented, and fines
assessed by the courts amounting to $3,000.

# SANITATION

## Extent of work

Approximately 36,000 inspections and 83,000
were made and 12,000 orders given by the sani
division during 1922. Investigations were mad
3,387 citizens' complaints. This is a decrease of
seven hundred complaints from the 1921 total.

ssity of keeping these places clean and free from
nin. Many rooming houses evade the city regula-
by being licensed under the state law as hotels
ough they do not strictly come under this
sification.

## ne work

reater control over home work was provided by a
enacted by the 1921 legislature requiring the em-
er to take out a license for each home in which
k is done. Before this license is issued, the home
t comply with the sanitary requirements of the
e board of health and the industrial commission.
number of new licenses issued in 1922 was 1708,
the number of home work inspections 5,058.

## ustrial sanitation

uch progress has been made in industrial sanita-
in the past few years, and fewer orders are neces-
each year. A number of the larger plants ap-
t a committee to inspect sanitary conditions
ughout the plant. This encourages each foreman
et his department in the best possible condition.

## tagious disease

he sanitary inspectors do practically all the quar-
ning and releasing of contagious disease work. This
k was increased during the year by epidemics of
oping cough and measles and the placarding of
ses for suspected contagious disease until it was
itely ascertained that the cases within either were
ere not measles. Contagious disease and placard-
calls were made in 25,000 cases. Cultures were
d for or delivered in 2,500 cases.

## ting of living quarters

he ordinance requiring a standard heat of seventy
ees Fahrenheit between the hours of 6:30 A. M.
10 P. M., when the temperature is below fifty de-
s Fahrenheit out of doors, was very well complied
during the year. A comparatively small number
omplaints were made. It is noticeable that when
plaints are made from apartment house dwellers,
are often made by all the dwellers instead of by
ngle one. Investigations are made only in case
omplaints. To check up on the heat provided by
landlord, a heat registering device is installed in
tenant's living quarters. In most cases a mere
ning to the landlord to provide more heat is suf-

located, were received. In cases where heat
nished by the landlord for violations of the h
dinance, if such occurred. In order to pro
pants of rented quarters who do their own l
is recommended that an ordinance be enacted
that heating systems shall be put in good wo
dition during the months from September to

## JOHNSTON EMERGENCY HOSPI

### Purpose and scope of work

The Johnston emergency hospital property
to the city by the late John Johnston to be m
for the care and treatment of emergency
accident and sickness. It is governed by a I
sisting of the commissioner of health and f
cians and three aldermen appointed by the n
is served by a staff of seventy-five physic
serve without compensation. Forty beds a
tained. Although operated as a charitable i
it is the policy of the hospital not to refuse
which may be presented to it.

### Work

During the past year 8,184 patients were
of whom 1,704 were women. This is an in
number of 451 over the number admitted
Eighty patients were dead upon reaching th
and one hundred and seven died in the hospi

An interesting phase of its work is the psy
ward which is maintained for observation
cases. The criminal courts and police departr
persons to this ward who are suspected of ha
tal abnormalities. A field nurse gets in to
the families or friends of the persons under
tion and prepares case histories for the use
ing alienists.

# CITY PLANNING

These include the acceptance of plats wit
miles of the city limits, the acquisition of lan
the civic center, street widening and gen
planning problems. The commission is al
tuted the real estate department of the cit
empowered with the consent of the common
act as its real estate agent in appraisal, a
transfer and sale of all real estate, other th
must, by law, be acquired by condemnation.

VIEW IN THE PROPOSED GROUP OF PUBLIC BUILDINGS MILWAUKEE 1922

it has taken in the past forty years, the
[ma]rk for population will be reached in 1975.
[develo]pment of the Milwaukee harbor with the
[larg]e shipping facilities on Lake Michigan
[prosp]ective development of the St. Lawrence
[a]ugurs well for a population which may
[be a m]illion and three-quarters by 1975.

[The] first steps in the program for the im-
[prov]ideration of the board of public land com-
[prise] that of zoning the outlying districts of
[...] Great industries are one of the sources
[of gr]owth and Milwaukee's future is directly
[tied i]n the future of its industries. The high-
[ways] from these industries and joining them
[in]dustrial and commercial centers are the
[...] through which the industrial and ac-
[...] must flow. In order that the city's
[futur]e provided for, the location of these in-
[dustri]ons must be judiciously planned. They
[need] room for expansion without crowding.
[be] so placed that once they have grown to
[proporti]ons the shipping of the commodities will
[be pro]vided for and will not blocked by their
[...] and lastly they must be near a railroad
[for] shipping to other cities economical. Co-
[in] the planning of these industrial centers
[is tha]n of thoroughfares, which must be of
[...] nd location as to carry the heavy traffic
[indu]strial center to another, or to shipping
[me]ans of a speedy and direct route. Suf-
[thorou]ghfares must be planned to take care of
[...] ty years hence. They must act as ar-
[teries] g and thereby relieving congestion on
[resi]dence and business streets and trans-
[port] ehicular traffic directly to its destination.
[It] is the locating of residential districts
[near th]ese industrial centers. Milwaukee is one
[of the] congested cities in the country. Only
[of the land within the city limits is now]

of Milwaukee built up with factories and the corres-
ponding necessary residential areas, both joined by
arterial thoroughfares, a large number of people may
work and live in the most ideal conditions.

Milwaukee county is planning a comprehensive
park and boulevard system, comprising over eighty
miles of park drives and many thousand acres of park
lands. Many of the small water courses, such as
Honey creek and Root River, are included in this park
system with the idea of conserving the natural beauty
and of aiding in the natural drainage of land, for if
such a plan of conserving the water sheds is not ad-
hered to, the alternative will be the building of miles
of expensive sewers. Milwaukee is most fortunate in
having in close proximity as beautiful a bit of country
as is to be found anywhere in the state. With the
view of making the most of this beauty, owners of
contiguous property are urged to pool their interests
as far as platting is concerned and engage the most
skillful professional assistance so as to do justice to
their opportunity. Subdivisions adjoining this park-
way are already being platted in accordance with this
idea, and the board believed that these better residential conditions will be eagerly grasped by prospec-
tive home builders. Inasmuch as this metropolitan
park system is soon to be a reality, it is most important
that a city park and boulevard system be so arranged
as to make the county park easily accessible from all
parts of Milwaukee. The third step, therefore, in the
program of the board of public land commissioners is
to make the city's park and boulevard system an ad-
junct to the splendid recreational areas which are soon
to surround the city.

It has been demonstrated in many large cities that
in addition to the major recreational areas there must
be small parks distributed over the city which may
be used as playgrounds or social centers or breathing
spots for those who cannot take the time to go to the
larger areas. Such smaller parks in London, are
known as "lungs", which term is rather descriptive
of their use. During the last year, the board of public

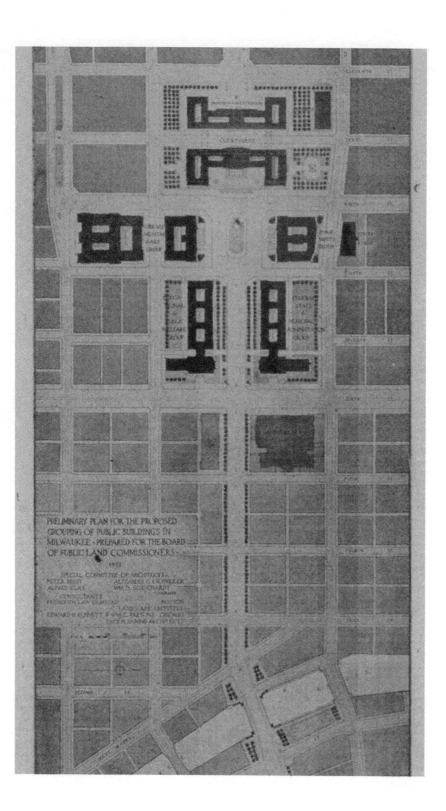

PRELIMINARY PLAN FOR THE PROPOSED
GROUPING OF PUBLIC BUILDINGS IN
MILWAUKEE · PREPARED FOR THE BOARD
OF PUBLIC LAND COMMISSIONERS ·
1922

ghway system, the study of street capaci-
pecial reference to automobile congestion,
ancing problems in connection with street
d the civic center, and in connection there-
reparation of bills to be presented to the
ture which will facilitate the procuring of
vements with the least burden on the tax

## r and Cedar-Biddle Street widening

rly months of 1922, prior to the spring
was deemed wise by the board to have the
e special committee of architects checked
trested and well-known city planning ex-
y, therefore, invited Mr. Frederick Law
Boston, and Messrs. Bennett and Parsons,
to carefully examine the project and give
as they deemed necessary. The general
special committee of architects was ad-
though some changes were made in detail.
rawings of the proposed civic center and
Cedar and Biddle streets were completed
end of March, 1922. Other than purchas-
ies along the Cedar-Biddle street widening
the civic center area, very little has been
l because sufficient power has not been
common council by state statutes to pro-
anner which would best protect the public
he needs of a growing city have heretofore
ciently understood by legislative bodies,
no permissive legislation has been enacted
e construction of hitherto unthought of
ts. Had the one-half mill tax been passed
pring election, considerable progress would
nade at a considerable saving of money.
hen adequate power has been granted the
he present state legislature, progress will
the actual achieving of the contemplated
t.

## department

ning of Cedar and Biddle streets and the
f enough land for the grouping of future
lings entails so much business that the
ncil has deemed it necessary to create a
estate department. This department oper-
the direction of the board of public land
rs. Since the creation of the department,
its work has considerably broadened and
been rendered to the county board of sup-
school board, the county park board, com-
public works, the tax department and the
ment.
l of public land commissioners, in accord-

real estate values and his general qualifications as
business-man made his acceptance of the office a matt
of great value to the city. During the year 1922, M
Grieb succeeded in obtaining for the city of Milwauke
offers of sale of property at or below the assess
valuation, amounting to $1,855,877. Of these offer
the council voted to purchase $867,365 worth of pro
erty. It is regretable that sufficient funds were n
at hand to purchase all of the offered properties, an
the fact that money enough was at hand to take a
vantage of these low prices, will prove costly. B
enough land has been bought to establish values whe
public improvements are contemplated and considerab
gain is made in that fact alone. The real estate d
partment also maintains the properties bought by th
city and has, at the present time forty-four building
in charge, all of which lie within the limits of the pr
posed civic center and Cedar-Biddle street projects.

## Annexation

During the past year, the board, with the assistan
of R. E. Stoelting, commissioner of public works, h
made considerable progress in annexation. A total
346.73 acres of land were annexed officially during th
year 1922. Petitions for additional 371.30 acres
land were passed and are now in the hands of the com
mon council. This area will officially become a part
Milwaukee, early in 1923. Petitions are now bei
circulated covering about 2,500 acres of land whic
should be ready for presentation to the council in th
near future. Efforts along this line are still hand
capped on account of water contracts, tax rates ar
large industrial concerns, but in spite of these di
ficulties, much has been accomplished in this directio
Physical growth, when not paralleled by corporate co
trol, results in lost opportunities for future ideal li
ing and working conditions and affects adversely bo
the city and the district obstructing annexation.

Although many plans have been made for the pr
jects stated above, Milwaukee is growing at such a ra
that the board of public land commissioners is fearf
lest the city will grow faster than these improvemen
may be made and earnestly urges the co-operation
all civic bodies, private as well as public, to the e
that the important phases of this program may be p
into effect before private improvements will have be
made, the removal of which will call for a vastly larg
expenditure of money. Milwaukee will be a very lar
city. Whether it will be a desirable city to live
lies very much in the hands of the people of toda
We are at the threshhold of important changes and
will require foresight, good judgment and courage
their part to make this city an acceptable heritage
future generations.

# PUBLIC WELFARE

## PARK BOARD

falk, president
stein
ndley
lak
eider

The board is vested with full and exclusive power
govern, manage and control and improve the city
parks, parked plots on boulevards, squares, triangl
and playgrounds, the lake shore drive and the zoo.
also has full power and authority over trees and shru
plantations between the lot line and curb of the city
streets and boulevards. A park police force is mai

Easter Lily Show, Mitchell Park Conservatory

ts and recreation. All work done on tree and shrub
tations between the lot line and the curb of the
streets, is assessed against abutting property,
pting that each year the common council allows an
ropriation for such overhead expenses as are not
ded in the assessments. Acquisitions of park lands
not made from this tax levy but are generally pro-
d for by bond issues.

### k property

he property under the jurisdiction of the board is
e hundred fifty acres in extent; three small parks
lucted in connection with the city water works
g the total city park property up to one thousand
es. Two of the parks, Lincoln, one hundred eighty
es in area, and Jackson ,eighty acres in area, are
side of the city limits. The park areas are forty-one
number of which fourteen range from thirteen to
hundred eighty acres in size; sixteen are small
ares and triangles, commonly known as breathing
ts, nine are parked center plots in boulevards and
are the reclaimed lands along the lake front.

he value of park property, based on the cost of land
l improvements, is over seven million dollars. The
ncipal addition to the park system for the year was
twenty acre tract acquired as an addition to
mboldt park. By this acquisition Humboldt park
s extended to the Bay View high school. Five lots
re acquired to secure a proper entrance to the
theast corner of Washington park. A number of
all areas were also added to the park system, among
m a gift of two acres for a recreation center in
Garden Homes housing dvelopment property.

### rk attendance

According to the estimates of the park police, over
million people visited the parks during 1922.
ashington park led with over a million visitors; Lake
rk was the next popular. There were over eight
ndred thousand visitors at the zoo. The atendance
the various recreation activities and celebrations is
follows:

| | |
|---|---:|
| Skating and skating events | 953,117 |
| Band concerts | 462,150 |
| Baseball | 314,254 |
| Flower shows | 238,760 |
| Sane Fourth celebrations | 206,000 |
| Swimming (Gordon and Lincoln parks) | 189,688 |
| Neptune frolic | 125,000 |
| Football | 117,120 |
| Tennis | 101,014 |

| | |
|---|---|
| Coasting and tobogganning | |
| Hockey | |
| Bowling on the green | |

### Park improvements

During the year a great many improven
made in the parks, the most important of
as follows:

A water system for the golf course and
pump to furnish the necessary water was i
Lincoln park.

Improvements were started on the squa
Sixteenth and Seventeenth, Finn and N
which was turned over to the board durin
year and which was in very bad shape.
large trees ranging from six to twelve inch
eter were planted inside the square and thi
inch elm and maple trees were planted i
border around the square.

Additional improvements were made i
park by grading and leveling, seeding ar
planting of trees and shrubs and the insta
sewer and water system. During the comi
northerly portion of the park will be put i
doing the necessary grading, installing a b
mond, tennis courts and children's play ap

The center plots in Sherman boulevard, f
to Burleigh streets have been improved
to subgrade, filling with black soil and
water sprinkling system. During the comi
will be completed by planting trees and
The completion of this boulevard to Bur
connects Sherman park with Washington

The principal improvement in Washingto
the construction of ten thousand square ya
Besides this, the piece of land at the nortl
of Fortieth and Vliet streets, turned over
during the last year for an easterly entran
ington park, was improved by doing th
grading, laying a water sprinkling syste
trees and constructing a walk.

The roadways in Kosciusko park were
provided with permanent tarvia pavement.
tennis courts were installed.

The border plantation in Humboldt pa
which was begun last year, was complet
shrubbery was planted in the grass plot
sidewalk and the curb.

The new additions in South Shore par
proved after the houses which were not
the city were removed, by necessary grad

ges or admission fees.

aring the summer season twenty-nine afternoon
l concerts and thirty-five evening concerts were
ided. These were rotated among six parks on a
ite schedule so that there was a concert in some
every week day evening and Saturday and Sun-
afternoons.

egularly scheduled amateur baseball games, 1028
umber, were played on the ball fields of four
s; 242 football games were played in five parks.
forty-one tennis courts, scattered in six of the
s, were used to capacity at all times. A nine hole
course in Lincoln park and a six hole golf course
ake park, furnished recreation to thousands of
rs of this game. In Lincoln and Gordon parks
ing and swimming facilities were provided. Dur-
the winter months ice skating was provided in nine
he parks and upon the upper Milwaukee river.
sting and tobogganing were provided in Lake, Wash-
on, Mitchell and South Shore parks. Horse racing
onducted at Washington park. Track and field
ts are held at Lake, Washington, Mitchell and
nboldt parks. Permits for picnics were issued to
groups, the largest of which were the annual labor
picnic given by the Federated Trades Council and
picnic of the Wisconsin Telephone Company's em-
es, both at Washington park. Neptune's Frolic,
ater carnival held on Lake Michigan just off Juneau
k, was instituted during the past year and proved
reat success. Sane Fourth of July celebrations and
works display were conducted in seven parks
ughout the city. Boating and canoeing is pro-
d for on the lagoons in Washington, Mitchell,
ciusko and Humboldt parks and on the Milwaukee
r. A new recreational activity instituted during
past year was outdoor dancing in Washington park.
s attraction was so successful that during the com-
year dancing pavilions will also be installed in
e of the other parks. The Washington park dances
e held on the second floor of the field building which
rlooks the lagoon and affords a dancing floor space
1,640 square feet. Dances were held every evening
epting Sunday and on Saturday afternoons. The
ning dances were arranged in two periods, from
0 to 9:30 and from 9:30 to 11:00. A charge of
cents for women and fifteen cents for men was
de for each period of dancing. This activity con-
ed for twelve weeks and had attendance of 42,179
and 40,337 women.

ublic recreational activities, not under the control of
park board, consists of supervised play on ten school
ygrounds and athletics in the social centers carried
under the direction of the school board. The pub-
bathing beaches at McKinley and South Shore parks
l the ice skating on flooded rinks on vacant lots scat-
ed over the city, are conducted by the department of
lic works.

## urist camp site

During the year a tourist camp site was established
the northwesterly part of Lake park. The camp
s opened on June 12, and closed on November
A total of 3,040 people comprising 885 parties
istored during this time. These parties came from

accordance with a plan adopted by the p
twelve year ago. The city maintains th
makes all improvements from the tax lev
therefor but the specimens, however, are
through the efforts of the Washington Park
Society, private donations and additions by
surplus animals are sold and the money rec
same is put into a fund with which othe
specimens are purchased. The exhibits
tracted much attention during the past yea
mother grizzly and her four cubs, and the
and her two cubs. The monkey island, a hill
feet in size and 35 feet high, is probably
popular attraction in the zoo area. The
surrounded by a moat filled with water, an
the monkeys range at will and delight th
visitors by their antics. Among recent ad
a male nubian lion, an India nylghai, a pair
saddle back tapirs, a pair fo Malayn bers
of South American condors.

## Conservatory

The conservatory at Mitchell park is one
places of the park system. Tropical plant
and beautiful flowers are always on exhi
annual chrysanthemum and easter lily
held at which thousands of these plants a
play. During the past year an electric li
tem was installed so as to allow the exi
be seen by night visitors.

## Lake front development

Milwaukee is one of the few lake-to-ocea
this country, if not the only one, which own
proportion of the property and riparian ri
her water front. The higher parts betwe
sin street and Lake park and between Rus
and the southern city limits are under the
of the park board, while the lower parts be
two strips are under control of the harbor
The area north of Lake park is still priva
An area of lake frontage, six hundred fee
and four thousand feet in length lying be
consin street and McKinley beach, has bee
for park purposes by the construction of a
water some distance from the shore line.
mound breakwater, five thousand feet in
one thousand feet from the shore line, ha
structed to protect the shore line from Rus
to the south city limits. The last five hund
this breakwater was completed in 1922.
been adopted for the construction of a driv
lake over this property from the head of M
to Lake park. Negotiations are now unde
the Chicago and Northwestern Railway C
the construction of a bridge over the rail
to connect the drive with the downtown po
city, based upon an agreement made fifty
when this company received its right of v

## Forestry work

The forestry division carries out the
planting of trees and shrubs, and the prun
ing, surgery work and the removal of al

nted on each street. The first tree in a block is
nty feet from intersection of curbs, and the
ance thirty to forty feet from each ohter according
the variety selected and is evenly distanced through-
the block. The two inch stem diameter is the stand-
l size tree planted. The price per tree, including the
noval of poor soil, replacing with good top soil,
ong stake, one inch mesh wire guard, hoops and ties,
5.25, the actual cost. The elm tree used is a grafted,
pendicular type, which is preferable to seedlings
ause seedings vary so greatly in form.

## TIZENS COMMITTEE ON UNEMPLOYMENT

J. Fairbairn, chairman
rry Lippert, secretary
s. E. E. Essman, assistant secretary

### ganization and duty

his committee was organized in 1912 primarily as
advisory board to the state industrial commission
operating the public employment offices in this city.
consists of twenty members, five aldermen chosen
the common council, five supervisors chosen by the
nty board of supervisors, five representatives of
ital chosen by the association of commerce and
representatives of labor chosen by the federated
des council. Its work is financed by appropriations
m the common council and the county board of su-
visors. It maintains a main office in the down town
tion of the city and a branch office on the south
e. Both men's and women's departments are main-
ned at the main office while the south side office is
casual laborers only. The men's department is
ided into clerical and professional, metal and build-
trades, miscellaneous trades, common labor, farm
or and handicap divisions, and the women's depart-
nt into clerical and professional, factory, hotel and
nestic service. (This makes it possible for the office
handle all types of people—technical and profes-
nal, skilled and unskilled. The office also co-operates
h the federal and state vocational boards.

### bor market

he labor market, like any other market, is con-
led by the law of supply and demand. At the be-
ning of 1922 it is estimated that there were 35,000
ple out of work, the demand for labor was practic-
at a stand still, and it was only through intensive
citing that jobs were found for the most needy.
the end of the year the labor situation was getting
k to normal again.

n the early part of the year many shops resorted to
rter working hours and to having their employes
k in shifts in order to keep as many workers on
r pay rolls as possible.

here was a turning point in the spring. The build-
industry commenced its activities sooner than
al, and with it, factories producing building facili-
showed a marked improvement. By May, road
struction had started and other industries as auto-
ile, textile, packing and shoe factories, increased
r number of workers and absorbed available labor.
many instances there was some difficulty in filling

placements in all divisions of the men's a
departments together with the large numl
porary placements from the Reed street o
the total to 66,310, which is the greatest
corded in any one year in the history of t

## GARDEN HOMES HOUSING DEVEL

### Garden Homes Company
Galbraith Miller, president
William H. Schuchardt, vice president
William D. Harper, secretary
Herman Fehr, treasurer

### What it is

The Garden Homes housing development
extension of the co-partnership method of
housing problem in the United States. T
was recommended by a housing commission
by the mayor a number of years ago after
gation of housing development in Europe an
Authority for cities and counties to invest
this type or housing corporation was gran
Wisconsin legislature in 1919. The Gard
Company was organized in 1920, and inve
fifty thousand dollars each were made by t
county of Milwaukee. A twenty-eight acr
land, just north of the city limits upon the
road and Atkinson avenue adjoining a stre
line, was secured. Upon petition, this trac
of the neighboring property was annexed
in order that it might be provided with city
nections, sewer facilities, street improve
playground, 250 by 600 feet given to the
hundred and sixty-five lots of a standard
by 160 feet an dover, but with many irregu
account of curving streets, were provided.

### Management

Management is vested in the hands of a b
rectors selected by the holders of both co
preferred stock on the basis of shares held.
as the preferred stock is retired control wil
in the holders of common stock. At this tin
holders will have an approximately equal sh
company as no one can own common stock i
the value of the house in which he is living.
and county each have representatives on th
directors, and the city's representative is
tary of the company.

### Stock

The capital stock of the company is fiv
thousand dollars, equally divided between
and common. Shares have a par value of
dred dollars. The preferred stock is held by
and draws interest at five per cent while th
stock is held by the occupants of the houses
interest only if the company so determine
vestments of fifty thousand dollars each th
county of Milwaukee each hold one-fifth o
ferred stock. The home occupant, instead
rent, makes a subscription, on the partia
plan, to the common stock amounting to th

alued at about $800, is about $4,300 and of a
house $4,700.  The maximum payment for a
house is about fifty dollars a month at the
t the end of twenty years when all interest
 preferred stock and amortization payments
eted, the payment will be a little less than

Of the 93 homes under construction, 78 will be c
pleted by May 1, 1923.  It is planned to have 105 ho
completed this year.  Fifty-nine house sites are a
able for future construction.  Five hundred app
tions for homes are on file.  Sixteen homes were
cupied by April 1, 1923.

# EDUCATION

## School Directors

H. Derse, president
ictor L. Berger
lora B. Bruins
 B. Charlton
Durand
ngeleke
e Esser
 F. Luehring
izabeth M. Mehan
Otjen
 Reiss
ell
V. Schnetzky
le Sherman
H. Zens

## committee on trade schools

 J. Neacy, chairman
uise M. Green
ph Raveret
arl Stern
re Trecker

## rative staff

 C. Potter, superintendent of schools
 E. Kagel, assistant superintendent
Theisen, assistant superintendent
et Canty, assistant superintendent
y Enderis, assistant to the superintendent
Lucas, assistant to the suprintendent
M. Harbach, secretary and business manager
 Anderson, auditor
F. Schroeder, supply clerk

## tration

blic school system is governed by a board
 directors of fifteen members elected at large
ters for six year terms.  The board is a con-
ody, five members of which are elected bien-
 reorganization of committees during the past
ced the number from seven to three—finance
ing, rules and complaints, and appointments
se of instruction.  A special executive com-
mposed of the president of the board and the
 of the committees on finance, rules and ap-
ts were created with power to act for the
emergency matters arising in the interim be-
ird meetings.

de schools are independently administered by
tee of five citizens appointed by the board of
rectors.

lucational activities are conducted under the

the board of estimates and the council if the approp
tions are within the mill tax limits provided by
statutes.  These levies total 7.8 mills and are div
as follows: maintenance, six mills; repairs, ei
tenths mills; trade schools, six-tenths mills; and
tension, four-tenths mills.  Additional revenues
be secured only by legislative sanction.

It is mandatory upon the common council to i
bonds for the acquisition of school grounds and
construction of school buildings up to one-fifth of
city's statutory debt limit.  However, the com
council may at its discretion authorize the levying
direct tax for this purpose in lieu of issuing bo
The policy of financing school construction from m
raised by direct taxation was inaugurated in the bu
for 1923 when the council granted the school boa
request to raise two hundred thousand dollars in
manner.

The budget allowance for public school purposes
1922 was $5,887,886; that for 1923 totals $6,247
Expenditures  for  educational  purposes  for
amounted to $6,523,415.  The fact that this am
exceeds the budget allowance is due to the inclu
of money raised by bond issues for school purp
Eighty-five per cent of the money raised by taxa
is used for the payment of salaries.

The per capita cost of education on an average m
bership basis is $66.76 for the elementary sch
$134.73 for the high schools, $145.06 for the g
trade school and $179.87 for the boys' technical
school.

## Educational equipment

The educational system includes seventy-six sch
valued at approximately twelve million dollars as
lows: six senior high schools, one technical high sc
one junior high school, one girls' trade school, one
vocational  school  and  sixty-six  elementary  sch
There are sixteen hundred class rooms in these b
ings.  The Grand avenue and Greenbush street g
mar schools, completed in 1921, and the Bay View
School completed in 1922 are model buildings.

## Building shortage and program

An acute school building shortage has been appa
for several years.  This is due largely to the
increase in school enrollment, the refusal of the fe
government to sanction building during the war
iod, high interest rates, increasing costs of mate
and a stationary debt limit.  In order to get de
information as to the extent of this shortage the fin
and buildings committee of the school board requ

nical high schools. The sites include nine
ary schools, five for junior high schools and
nior high schools. Only eight of these will
in the five year period, but the acquisition
r seven, which include sites for the future
schools, is recommended as these buildings
ded in the near future and their purchase
le at the present time at reasonable figures.
provision is made for playgrounds in the
new school buildings, but no provision is
adly needed additional playground space in
ted districts of the city because to do so
o increase the cost of the program $500,000
icipated revenues.

of the program will be $6,600,000 of which
is the cost of new buildings and $600,000 of
The recommendations are that $3,600,000 of
be raised from bond issues during the next
that $1,400,000 now in the treasury be used
the common council be requested to raise
nnually by direct tax from 1924 to 1927

e present shortage in school buildings has
zed and school building needs become more
t is suggested that school buildings be
y direct taxation and that bond issues be
only for extraordinary expenses such as the
high schools.

e of interest to note that in the last decade
omplete buildings have been erected, three
ls and eleven modern grammar schools. In
l also all buildings in the city except three
completely renovated and modernized, and
the remaining three are now under way.
f this work was foreseen several years ago
gislature was asked to increase the tax levy
for this purpose from three to eight-tenths

This was granted and approved by the
in a popular referendum. The levy yields
hundred thousand dollars annually.

thorough survey of necessary alterations and
as made during the year by the city fire and
spection departments.

## staff

ervisory force consists of the superintendent
, three general assistants and directors and
s of industrial education, drawing, ele-
manual training, household arts, physical
music, special classes and welfare depart-

manent teaching force includes eighteen hun-
ons. Of these seventy-five are principals,
ers in high schools, 1,028 teachers in grades,
rgarten teachers, and 124 teachers of manual
domestic art, special classes and defective

rs in Milwaukee are favored with permanent
id a minimum-maximum salary scale which
zed as the highest in the United States. As
the annual turnover in the teaching force is
five per cent.

Its purpose is to give the teachers an opportunity
express themselves on current educational probl
and to assist in their solution. The council wo
through small steering committees selected by its p
ident and sub-committees of as many members
deemed desirable selected from the teachers at la
Meetings of the council are held monthly. The com
tee on projects and games for primary grades, in
junction with one of the assistant superintendents,
pared a pamphlet upon that subject which was pri
for school use. The various projects and games v
tried out, and the pamphlet is now being revi
Other committees have been studying thrift educat
history and reading work, teaching of physiology
hygiene in the grades, teaching of safety and
development of closer co-operation between parents
teachers.

## School census

The annual school census taken in the early par
the year revealed a population of 138,955 person
school age, an increase of more than five thousand
that of the year before. These are practically ev
divided between boys and girls. Of these 62,878
69.4 per cent were enrolled in the public schools
27,761 in the private and parochial schools.

## Attendance

The school year opened with a registration of 64
in comparison to 62,020 for the previous year.
December the enrollment had increased to 65,31
comparison to 62,843 for the previous year. Of t
9,400 are in the high school, 48,000 in the gra
7,400 in the kindergartens and 400 in the trade cla
In the last ten years the public school enrollment
increased 48.4 per cent in comparison with a 22.2
cent increase in population during the interval
tween the last two federal census enumerations.
greatest increase has been in the high schools w
the enrollment has increased more than 135 per cer
comparison with a 40 per cent increase in the
mentary schools.

## Crowded schools

The great increase in school attendance witho
proportionate increase in building accommodations
led to the overcrowding of many of the schools
classes. This has necessitated the housing of cl
in barracks, the inauguration of half day classes
use of assembly rooms as class rooms, and the inc
in the size of the classes. Forty-three barracks
in connection with twenty-one schools house tw
five hundred pupils. Over two thousand pupil
tend school on a half-time basis, over one thousan
housed in assembly rooms and one hundred in base
rooms. Thirty-two manual training and cooking
ters are located in basements, four in assembly
and one in a barrack.

Over-crowded conditions are also shown by the
that many classes include forty-five or more p
per teacher, which is a greater number than a
should contain to get the best results.

organization of kindergarten bands, construction
large blocks, and the utilization of all available
e as playrooms.

## ic

he teaching of music and musical appreciation is
in in the kindergartens and continued throughout
school course. In the last semester of 1921-2
e was an enrollment of thirteen hundred in the in-
mental music classes. The violin was the most
ilar instrument, and one thousand children were
lled in classes studying this instrument while
e hundred were studying cornet, flute, trombones,
horns, clarinets, drums and other instruments.
lessons are given in a ten week term at a total
nse of $1.50 to the student.

uring the first half of the 1922-3 eight bands coming two hundred twenty-five pupils, were organized.
ee represented one school while five were formed
more than one school. The band members are boys
girls from eight to thirteen years old and from the
th to eighth grades. Band books are furnished by
board of education. Practice sessions are held
ng the noon recess. Band members are expected
practice thirty minutes daily and to exercise the
cles of their mouths each day.

lthough the band members know very little of
ic when organized, the music director hopes to
the individual bands to a state of proficiency
re they can be assembled into one large band

## vocational school

he prevocational school, established early in 1922,
ow housed in four barracks, containing both class
work rooms, on Kosciusko square. It is designed
serve boys who have been refused general labor
nits on account of the lack of the proper educational
irements. Each of the boys in this school had fall-
from one to three years behind in the school cur-
lum on account of lack of interest in his studies.
this school the boys are divided into particular
ups according to their individual ability irrespective
ge and prepared for a vocational career. All sub-
s are interpreted in the light of utility as a means
leveloping a foundation for academic training.

## eet trades

order to control delinquency and incorrigibility
ng newsboys, the legislature has made it mandatory
them to attend school and to satisfy the school
horities that they are physically and mentally able
do such work besides their ordinary school work.
s is controlled by a permit system administered by
school authorities.

o better regulate street trade matters there has
n organized what is known as the Newsboys' Re-
lic. The organization is democratic, and self gov-
ment prevails. Officers are elected annually. A
rsboys' trial board handles cases of violations of
street trades law, many of which would subject
offender to being brought into municipal court.

including three high schools. Over thirty-fi
persons were enrolled in evening activities i
schools, and forty-seven hundred in the grad

## Citizenship classes

The Americanization classes, held at twe
schools, are particularly interesting. Here,
wish to become citizens are found striving t
intricacies of the English language. Beside
es in the schools, morning classes were hel
trial plants and special classes in the even
settlement house and one parochial school.
for foreign women were also conducted und
ervision of the school authorities at the Ab
coln house. Upon completing the course a
tion as to knowledge of the American gov
given by the naturalization examiners of
States department of labor. Those passi
amination are given diplomas certifying t

## Athletics

Amateur athletics in the city have been f
greatly extended by the school authorities.
director of athletics has been in active char
tically all organized amateur sport. Durin
season there were organized under his gui

| | |
|---|---|
| 52 baseball leagues | 6,160 registe |
| 10 basketball leagues | 888 registe |
| 7 football leagues | 1,240 registe |
| 1 soccer league | 168 registe |
| 1 hockey league | 94 registe |
| 4 athletic meets | 492 entries |
| 10 skating meets | 2,608 entries |
| 4 swimming meets | 398 entries |

During the summer the city had to b
combed for places where baseball games
played.

Supervised play is conducted during th
months on fourteen playgrounds, equippe
necessary playground apparatus and fac
amusements. Fourteen track, field, swim
canoe meets were conducted, in one of whic
was eligible to compete by simply making
at any playground. First aid instruction
at eight of the playgrounds and folk danc
at eight.

## LOCAL BOARD OF INDUSTRIAL ED

James D. Hickey, president
O. A. Muehl, secretary
A. J. Lindemann
Christopher Scholka
Milton C. Potter
Robert L. Cooley, director of vocational ed

## Organization and control of vocational

The local board of industrial education
two employers of labor and two employes, v
superintendents or foremen, appointed by
of school directors in charge of the full t

d three practical farmers appointed by the
a member of the industrial commission ap-
the commission, and the state superintendent
. Active charge of the state work is vested
director of vocational education and field
nted by the board.

anization of both local and state boards and
of vocational instruction is provided for by
Cities with a population of over five thousand
s are compelled to provide for a local board
rial education while cities with a population
an five thousand inhabitants are permitted

## the board

isconsin statutes provide that it is the duty
al board "to establish, foster and maintain
schools for instruction in trades and in-
ommerce and household arts in part-time day,
d evening classes" and such other branches of
are enumerated in other sections of the

## ral continuation and vocational school

liance with the statutory mandate, the board
lished continuation or vocational classes for
and girls and adults. For a period of ap-
ly ten years these classes had been held in
rters, but, very early in the existence of these
was determined to centralize all work. Ac-
plans for the construction of a central con-
and vocational school building were drawn
he present building at Seventh and Prairie
s erected. Classes were transferred to this
arly in 1923.

tral school is a model of its kind and has
y praised by educators from all parts of this
nd Europe. The idea of centralizing educa-
cations in a single school is well established
, but, in Milwaukee, it was possible to go a
er and centralize all the vocational groups in
ng with the result that there is greater flexi-
adaptibility in meeting educational demands
n it.

tral school is six stories high, covers ground
,940 square feet, contains 158 class and in-
rooms. Its cost was in the neighborhood of
n dollars. A kitchen and lunch service is
d which serves one hundred instructors and

by the school are turned out by boys learning
printing trade. One of the most complete elect
shops in the city is maintained for persons stud
the electrical courses. Apparatus for a complete
foundry course is being installed in one of the r
Rooms, with the necessary machines and equipmen
the study of household arts are provided. In fac
school is designed to be a complete business college
boys and girls who are compelled to leave schoo
the various vocations and crafts represented in
business and industrial life of the city.

## Finances

Like the board of school directors, the local boar
industrial education is an independent board ha
a mill tax of not to exceed one and one-half mills
levying of which is mandatory upon the common c
cil upon certification by the board. The erectio
the central continuation school has, however,
financed by the issuance of bonds by the common c
cil, but the sinking fund and interest upon these b
are payable from the board's tax levy.

The state of Wisconsin is permitted by statu
appropriate not to exceed thirty thousand dollars
nually toward the cost of salaries for instruction
supervision of the local school. The state also
vides funds toward the promotion of vocational
habilitation of persons disabled in industry or ot
wise.

Federal tuition is given for the vocational trai
of disabled soldiers of whom there are about
hundred in daily training.

## Function of the school

It is the function of the school to intelligently
cover, promote and aid in satisfying the educati
needs of the young people of the city who are not
tending the regular full time schools. The bulk of
toilers, and many others, acquire what they do acq
by the process of learning while earning. The f
tion of this school is to put system and order into
"'learn while you earn" processes. The word "
tinuation" expresses the idea of the school which
enable the person who is forced to leave the gr
full-time school to continue his training and educa

## Compulsory school attendance

All persons between the ages of fourteen and six
who have not the equivalent of a high school educa

to attend four hours per week during the first
ears of their apprenticeship regardless of age.

re are approximately thirty thousand young peo-
 Milwaukee between the ages of fourteen and
 years not attending school and largely em-
. It is figured that about 15,000 or more of these
under the compulsory part time attendance law
re required to attend the continuation school a
um of eight hours per week.

## ilitation of the handicapped

onsibility for the rehabilitation of the handicap-
hether injured while employed or at other times
ices is a special function of the continuation
 with the aim of re-educating him to overcome the
ap for an occupation in which the handicap will
event him from earning a decent living.  State
isors under the state board actively co-operate
pervise this work which receives both federal and
id.

e the war there have been a number of injured
s in attendance taking vocational training at
pense of the federal government.

## e of study

course of study presents about one hundred sub-
n the day and night courses.  The division into
ts is not an arbitrary one but is flexible so as
t any condition or demand even in the middle of
hool year.  The subjects are generally of a prac-
ocational character.

day course contains such courses as architectural
ng, automobile mechanics, blacksmithing, book-
g, bricklaying, cobbling, concrete work, drug
g, electric wiring, housekeeping, masonry,
ery, mechanical drawing, painting, plumbing,
g, stenography, tailoring, tool making, watch-
g and welding.

night course contains interesting courses in
ectural design, arithmetic, bookkeeping, cooking,
aking, engineering principles, gas engines, heat
ent of steel, illuminating engineering, income
nterior decorating, millinery, pharmacy, shop
nics, Spanish, structural drafting and window
ng.

nany cases the same subjects are taught in both
nd night courses, but, as attendance at night
s is voluntary and extends to adults, the night
 contains a wider range of business and man-
nt subjects.  The day courses for the younger
ts do not aim to teach a trade but rather to
kill in handling tools and to aid in the selection
rade or vocation.  It teaches them the value of
ring early in life for the work they are to do
they are grown up.

 great flexibility of the course of instruction is
ated by the request of the retail meat dealers of
ty for a night course in meat merchandising after
aw the improvement of their butcher's assistants
ere attending the compulsory day-time classes.

ers

bookkeeping, 28 in cafeteria classes.  Of the 
in the permit division, 936 were studying home
ics, 280 machine shop, 242 bookkeeping, 196 el
104 cabinet-making, 98 in printing and the 
miscellaneous craft classes.  Of 509 apprenti
were enrolled in the general apprentice divis
the rest in miscellaneous crafts.  One hund
ninety persons are enrolled in the rehabilita
vision.  There were 5,836 adults in attendance
classes held in seven school buildings scatter
the city.

## Placement of students in jobs

While the school does not guarantee jobs for
dents, it does maintain an employment departn
very many of its unemployed pupils.  Since th
lishment of this department it has had more g
to offer than boys and girls to fill them.  Firs
it helps the pupils to remain employed and, i
this, the feeling is that any work that does n
fere with the health or morals is better than
at all.  But the school itself goes further th
in that it helps the pupil in picking out a vocat
will earn him substantial wages after he has gr

# PUBLIC LIBRARY

## Board of trustees

## Governing authority

The Milwaukee public library is governe
board of trustees of nine members, consisting
citizens, one named each year for a term of fou
and three aldermen appointed by the mayor, a
of the school board appointed by the board
superintendent of schools.

## Extent of service

Every inhabitant of Milwaukee, whether ma
an or child, owns a book at the public libra
there are now more books in the library th
are inhabitants in the city.  Every family in
upon the average, possesses a borrower's ca
there are about 100,000 families in Milwau
the library has issued over 100,000 borrower
Every family in the city borrows, upon the
approximately one book every two weeks, s
library has circulated approximately 2,500,00
during the year, which is twenty-five books
family.  It is true, of course, that not ever

Library-Museum Building

Of these, 871 are in the schools, both grade
[par]hial; 129 of the collections are outside the
[cen]tered throughout the county. This county
[is] rendered under a contract by which the coun-
[ty pays t]he city a reasonable sum for each book cir-

[The gr]eat number and wide distribution of places
[where boo]ks are available makes Milwaukee county one
[of the mo]st admirably served counties in the United
[States fr]om the standpoint of accessibility of books
[to the rea]der. Every resident of the county is within
[walking d]istance of a public library station. This
[service is] supplemented by a parcel post service di-
[rected to t]he homes of county residents living outside
[the limits] of the city of Milwaukee.

## [Extent o]f service

[That th]e library is a constantly increasing factor
[in commu]nity life is shown by the following statistical
[compariso]n of the main items of its service for 1921

| | 1922 | 1921 |
|---|---|---|
| [Books i]n the library | 495,152 | 453,396 |
| [Readers]' cards in use | 105,759 | 94,715 |
| [Circ]ulation | 2,474,770 | 2,155,739 |
| [Book] collections in city | | |
| [and c]ounty | 1,122 | 779 |

[These f]igures show approximately a ten per cent
[increase in] the number of books in the library, in the
[number of] persons using these books and in the num-
[ber of boo]ks circulated and a forty per cent increase
[in the num]ber of book distributing centers.

## [What peo]ple read

[It is enc]ouraging to note that there has been a steady
[increase i]n the percentage of non-fiction books drawn
[from the] library to the total number of books drawn
[during th]e past decade. Considering the great in-
[crease in] circulation, this would seem to indicate that

lence. Much of the material is of the kind that
a constantly increasing monetary value and ten ye[ars]
from now will be impossible to secure. The select[ions]
were personally made from lists prepared in the o[wn]
department by a well known librarian who spent [a]
summer in Europe purchasing for several la[rge]
libraries.

## Service to the business world

The business man is just awaking to the fact t[hat]
library service is a great asset to his business. Thi[s is]
indicated by the fact that many large business hou[ses]
are attaching themselves to the public library by [in-]
stalling collections of library books for the use [of]
their staff. These include fiction as well as techn[ical]
and non-fiction books. The worker has his choice [of]
reading what he wishes; but, if he wants a book [to]
help him increase his value to his employer, the [op-]
portunity of doing so is presented to him.

The library collection of technical and scien[tific]
works is being constantly extended. Research w[ork]
in both the science and reference room is encoura[ged]
and every effort is made by the attendants in t[hese]
rooms to be of assistance in this work. The tran[sfer]
of the technical periodicals to the science room, earl[y in]
1923, was a step in the direction of making the [li-]
brary more useful to the technical man.

Books on the various trades and crafts are be[ing]
purchased constantly so that the library can meet [the]
demands of artisans who will wish to increase t[heir]
knowledge of their trades. Lists of craft books h[ave]
been distributed to the various trade unions.

## Service to the municipal authorities

Through the municipal reference library in the [city]
hall, the public library endeavors to give practical [as-]
sistance to the municipal authorities. This service [may]
take the form of securing data upon traffic regulat[ion]
of other cities for a member of the common council,

library is much used by the schools, civic or-
ions and individuals interested in civic prob-
Its pamphlets and clipping files contain excel-
terial upon the conduct of municipal affairs.

## al service

he leading hospitals are now periodically visited
ember of the library staff, the hospital librarian,
ery patient in the hospital, who is able to read,
viewed and given an opportunity to secure the
desires. The service is a real bed side service
books are brought to the patient in the wards
the private rooms on a wheel-truck. Requests
om fairy tales for children, technical books for
lled artisan, books in native languages for for-
, western and detective stories for the men, light
and books on household arts for the women.
service has received the highest co-operation
mmendation of hospital officials and doctors who
ze that books constitute a therapeutic instru-
ity of the greatest benefit to the convalescent.
ospital book drive in June resulted in the gift
sands of excellent books and magazines for this
y the citizens of the city.

## ance in adult education

part that the public library serves in education
of the general circulation of books is reflected
number of classes which meet in the library
Preference is given to purely educational activi-
the assignment of rooms available for gather-
Classes of the University of Wisconsin exten-
ivision and workers' college are held in the
g almost daily. The auditoriums of the south
id Llewellyn branches have been greatly in
l.

great number of special classes, held both with-
library building and without, made it advisable
loy a supervisor of adult education. The work
s the bring-
library serv-
adults in the
iation school
, extension
ening classes
school board,
's c l u b s,
es, Y o u n g
i's Christian
ation, a n d
s of Colum-
isses, the uni-
ity extension
vorkers' col-
roups of adult
ts and many
ellaneous
The local
is the first
e country to
the need of
ied worker to
these people
inding o u t

ped at the end of the year. The school librarian
allowed to elect as to whether they should rer
the library service or transfer to the school s
Two of them elected to stay with the library and
to transfer to the school system.

## Special services

The library serves the public in other ways t
the loan of books:

The weekly story-hour in the young people's
is proving attractive to many children; the
collection of piano-player rolls, chiefly classic sel
of educational value, is altogether insufficient t
the demand; the collection of pictures has been
stant circulation to schools, stores, factories a
vertising agencies.

The club room and lecture room have been
much demand that many applications have had
refused, and the auditoriums in two branch lik
South side branch and at Llewelyn branch i
View, have been almost equally in demand.

## Informing the public of the usefulness library

The library has developed a richness in its res
that is unappreciated by the general public.
these resources at command the library problem
largely, therefore, a question of informing the
that the library is prepared to serve. This has
a program of publicity in which the library ha
generously supported by many of the organizatic
institutions of the city, the newspapers, of
leading in the assistance which they have re
Even the radio is called upon to broadcast books

The library has been systematically studying
and devising new methods of calling the atten
the public to these resources. The frequently c
sidewalk signs, in front of the building, are a
this program
select collecti
books lining
walls of the
ery room are
er means of
ing the rea
borrow usefu
cultural book
numerous si
the library
ings are al
this purpose.

Select boo
upon subjects
terest are co
ly being co
and widely
uted. In
out these lis
continuation
h a s co-o
splendidly i
tributing.

lower books was made, and hundreds of
plant catalogs were given away in connec-
e fall flower show held in the lobby of the
um building. Children's book week was
of a large display of children's books in
peoples' room and in the branch libraries.
its and posters were placed in the windows
lown town stores, calling attention to the


vork by its very nature demands highly
kers. It has outgrown the stage where the
on of the librarian was to sit behind a
check out books. The local institution re-
s situation and is making every effort to
iff to do better work. Employes are freely
of absences to attend educational institu-
ral are now attending normal schools, uni-
d library schools. For each of the past
six members of the staff have attended the
mmer session of the University of Wiscon-
school with no deduction in pay for the
ourteen members of the staff attended the
ibrary Association meeting at Detroit last
d nine of them were enrolled in the course
on on library publicity at the expense of
ibrary.
taff luncheons have been held in all but the
months. These luncheons bring the staff
frequent intervals, and tend to develop a
t de corps among its members. On the av-
ibly of once a month speakers are invited
nt to give the staff benefit of their knowl-
special subjects. Reviews of the current
fiction and non-fiction, are frequently given
of the book selection department. A nom-
of twenty-five cents is made to persons
he luncheon, and this more than covers all


staff meetings of department heads are
over library problems and to devise better
doing library work. These meetings have
tive of much good to the library.

## PUBLIC MUSEUM

ation
ic museum is administered by a board of
mprised of three aldermanic and four citi-
rs, appointed by the mayor. To these are
ex-officio members, the superintendent of
the president of the school board or some

000; of its collection of specimens, $575,000; of i
museum reference library, containing 30,716 entri
$31,440; of the lantern slide collection, most of wh
are colored, $32,142; making a total valuation
$1,516,582.

## General range of collections and exhibits

The museum embraces a very wide range of
hibits and activties. The arrangement of the exhib
which will serve to show their extent, is as follows:

First floor
  Anthropology
    Geological history of
      man
    Archaeology
    Ethnology
      Ethnology groups
    History
      Historical groups
    Nunnemacher collec-
      tion
      Numismatics
      Musical instrument
      Arms and armor
      Lighting devices
      Bronzes, ivories,
      etc.

  Ceramics
  Children's room

Second floor
  Foreign ethnology
    Birds
      Bird groups
    Mammals
      Mammal groups

Third floor
  Marine invertebrates
  Reptiles and batrach
  Fishes
  Mollusks
  Insects
  Botany
  Geology

## Work in Anthropology

In the department of anthropology various re
rangements have been made in the anthropological a
historical exhibits, as well as several additions to
Nunnemacher collection.

Anthropological field work has been carried on amc
the Sauk, Kickapoo, Ioway and Oto Indians of Ok
homa, from whom extensive collections, represent
the daily life, costumes and religion of these tri
have been gathered, as well as a large amount of d
referring to their culture.

Among the more interesting specimens collected a
now mostly on exhibition, were fourteen sacred v
bundles or portable shrines of the Sauk, in which w
many beautiful antique articles, such as head dress
garments, prisoner ties, human scalps and the li
which are exceedingly rare and valuable. From
Ioway tribe were obtained all the tribal peace pip
beautiful specimens with carved effigy bowls of st
and stems ornamented with the skins and heads
rare birds and the dyed quills of the porcupine. N
of these Ioway pipes are in the possession of any ot
museum in the world.

The department has also been enriched by seve
notable gifts, among which was the G. E. Copel
collection, containing among other things, the b
series of stone implements from Hawaii, now in
United States.

## Groups and murals

The department groups and murals has opened th
large environmental groups during the year. One
these depicts the storming of Chapultepec, in
Mexican war and another, the Battle of Winches
depicting Sheridan's ride of the civil war period.
third group, depicts a buffalo drive among the Bla

Historical Groups, Public Museum

additions have been made to the herbarium
partment of botany, through field trips, par-
in southwestern Wisconsin, during the sum-
in Shawano county.

## nmal exhibits

ebrae zoology, improvements have been made
lections, but the greater amount of the time
rkers in this department has been spent in
ration of material for the building of a new
habitat groups of birds and mammals. Most
hong these is the securing by a museum ex-
f the materials for a representation of the
annet meeting colony on Bonaventure island
of St. Lawrence.

museum had the good fortune to secure,
e generosity and co-operation of the Colorado
f natural history in Denver, seven excellent
of elk, which will be used in building a large
in our mammal series.

## l expeditions and groups

ion to various marked improvements in the
l collections of the department of geology,
ucted during the last summer, two important
One for the purpose of selecting the ma-
data for the glacier group and the other for
purpose, showing the results of water
or these two groups, which are to form the
large series of environmental groups, Nis-
ier, and the south-slope of Mount Rainier,
rand canyon in Arizona were chosen as
jects.

the co-operation and financial assistance of
kee road, the Mount Rainier National Park
nd the Santa Fe railway, these two groups
ossible. The large cases required for the
t of these groups are now being erected in
l.

tion with the field work in vertebrate zoo-
geology, the museum has maintained two
ure cameras for considerable periods in the
the result that many thousands of feet of
ave been secured, showing most interesting
the bird colony on Bonaventure island and
eresting features of the geology of the
ier region and of the Grand canyon of

## rk

does the museum assemble as far as pos-
n collections by direct field work, but its
v build all groups, models and other items
install all exhibits. Exhibition cases are
in the museum's own shop, and the power
hes light, heat and power for both the
l the public library. The service rendered
y is on a strictly cash basis.

## service

n to its exhibits, in which environmental
strongly emphasized, the museum main-

## Children's room

On Christmas day, 1921, the museum opene
children's room, where special exhibits and instru
of interest to the young are at all times found
which is presided over by a woman docent. This
proven during the last year a great pleasure and
cational benefit to the many children who are
in many cases, given their introduction to science
nature study.

## Reference library

The museum's reference library, which is m
tained primarily as a working library for the s
but which is also available to students, now comp
30,176 entries consisting of 12,290 volumes and 18
pamphlets. During the year 1922, there were a
to th elibrary 797 volumes and 260 pamphlets.

## Attendance

As the time goes on, the museum's function in
community is becoming more and more thoroughly
derstood and greater numbers of Milwaukee's citi
are availing themselves of the great educational
portunities offered by this institution, through its
exhibits, its groups, its lectures and other exten
activities. During the year 1922 about 600,000 v
tors sought instruction in the exhibition halls
about 150,000 attended its various lecture courses.
these about 58,000 were school children of the f
to the eighth grades, who come for special instruc
in natural science subjects. This is done as a regu
part of their school work. Somewhat over 30,000 ad
attended the Sunday lecture course and other thousa
came to the Wednesday courses and to the Satur
lectures and field trips.

All these lectures are given by the museum staff,
cept those of the Sunday course. These are given
the best professional lecturers procurable from
parts of the country. At first they were given only
Sunday afternoon, but, when the course grew so po
lar that it became necessary, after filling the la
lecture hall to its utmost capacity, to turn away
many as five hundred persons, it was deemed advisa
to have each lecture repeated in the evening. T
has proven eminently successful for the past th
seasons, as the above mentioned attendance figu
show.

## Extent of collections

The museum's collection comprises the following:

| | |
|---|---|
| Mammals | 3,6 |
| Birds | 14,0 |
| Birds' eggs and nests | 6,6 |
| Reptiles and batrachians | 2,2 |
| Fishes | 4,2 |
| Insects | 103,5 |
| Mollusks | 106,4 |
| Crustaceans | 1,5 |
| Radiates, protozoans, etc | 1,9 |
| Fossils | 19,9 |
| Minerals and rocks | 13,9 |

| | |
|---|---|
| Collected in the field by the staff | 3,650 |
| Purchased | 548 |
| Made in the laboratories of the museum | 82 |
| Exchanged for duplicate material | 55 |

# MILWAUKEE AUDITORIUM

litorium board
ity representatives
Daniel W. Hoan
John I. Drew, treasurer
Louis M. Kotecki, secretary
John M. Niven
William Kaumheimer
George A. West

lirectors Milwaukee Auditorium company
William George Bruce
Oliver C. Fuller
Alvin P. Kletzsch, president
Otto J. Schoenleber
Emil H. Ott

eph C. Grieb, manager

### nership of building and site

he Milwaukee auditorium is owned jointly by the
of Milwaukee and the Milwaukee Auditorium com-
y. This company included 2,663 stockholders orig-
lly, representing 25,000 shares with a par value
en dollars. The city of Milwaukee originally was
er of a half interest which, however, has been in-
sed by the gift of shares from the individual stock-
ers.

he auditorium site is owned by the city, one-half
he result of a gift from Byron Kilbourn, the other
by purchase in 1880. The building was erected
cost of $661,000, of which $314,000 was contrib-
by the city.

### nagement

he auditorium management is vested in a board of
en members, six of whom hold office by virtue of
ial positions in the city government and five of

### Building

The structure occupies a city block. Its
clude a main arena, a sub-ground-level hal
smaller halls. Due to its remarkable flexi
building has been able to adequately house
of public gathering for which it has been ca
Entertainments, conventions, religious ser
military drills have been held simultaneou
its roof without conflict and with perfect
each.

The main arena has a seating capacity of
six smaller halls, a combined capacity of 5
sub-ground-level hall is used for exhibits
and is not equipped with seats, and covers
the entire ground area of the building.

### Finances

The auditorium has been self-sustaining
inception. It neither accumulates nor distri
fits, however. For the year ending Septembe
it showed an income of $150,000 and expen
$106,000. The surplus was set aside in a re
in anticipation of the board's program for
ments.

In aid of conventions and to encourage thei
in Milwaukee the city appropriates annua
cover hall rentals for convention authorities.
propriations in the 1923 budgets are $9,500

In the spring eelction of 1923, a bond issue
000 was voted to make extensive alterations,
a new roof, additional electrical equipment,
acoustics, a State street entrance to Planki
and renovation and redecoration. Although
torium might have financed these improvem
its current revenues, technicalities necessitat
icipal bond issue, the principal and interest
will be paid from auditorium revenues durir
of the bonds.

### Use, 1922

The following record of hall uses indicates
ities of the auditorium in 1922:

| | |
|---|---|
| Industrial and educational | |
| —Concerts and dances | |

of some of the important events in 1922 sea-

—Automobile show, national convention of
ng fixtures manufacturers.
y—Wisconsin retail hardware dealers,
rs' circut.
-Grand opera, style week show.
Bull fight, dances of Boston store employes,
marching club and Moose.
hriners ball.
Convention of world's advertising clubs, radio

—Food and household show, fall festival of
loose.
er—Wisconsin teachers' association conven-

er—Wisconsin implement show, Wisconsin
cts exposition.

## 1923

the auditorium opened its season with the
ntinuous use of the main area in its history.
was converted to the use of the American
Congress, twenty-eight alleys being installed
-five successive days of bowling being en-
During the year, the American mining con-
Grand Army of the Republic, the Wisconsin
xposition, the national poultry show and a
of similar large and important events are
The building is showing a gradually in-
se and a continuously wider service to Mil-
d the outside public.

## IILWAUKEE ART INSTITUTE
### Trustees

waukee art institute is organized for the
encouraging the fine and applied arts; to
the love of beauty and to cultivate the
e, and in that behalf to establish and main-
lleries, expositions, schools and any requis-
ul institutions; to obtain, by purchase, gift
intings and other works of art.

## ment and growth

sand, later to fifteen thousand and in 1922 to t
thousand dollars. Meanwhile, the institute bu
had outgrown its use and equipment in every wa;
had to be remodeled. Extensive changes were
and the remodeled building was opened to the
in March, 1922.

The building, as remodeled, contains on the g
floor the art library, the children's room and a spa
gallery devoted to constantly changing exhibitio
Wisconsin art where artists of the state may place
works at any time; on the first floor an entrance
which will be used as a gallery for bronzes, an
torium seating three hundred persons and fitted
a stage suited to the presentation of miniature
a front exhibition gallery for exhibits of various s
and on the second floor a large exhibition g
thirty-eight feet by seventy equipped with the
improved daylight lighting effects, a second gallery
a print room.

## The city contract

The grant of twenty thousand dollars in 1922
conditioned upon the fact that a contract be en
into, which was negotiated signed by the institute
the city in April, 1922, whereby the city should ac
an annual equity and in ten years complete owne
of the building, its furnishings, equipment and v
of art of which the institute was absolute own
which might be donated to it in the future. The
agreed to appropriate not less than twenty thou
dollars to it annually and to assume payment o
remaining one-half of a twenty year installment
gage of forty thousand dollars which would be
standing at the time the city takes full possessio
the institute. The city further agreed to approp
to the institute after it becomes the property of
city a sufficient sum "to carry on the work now
ried on by the institute and such as shall be ne
for the normal development of its activities and
mensurate with the increased educational and
mercial necessity arising out of the growth of the c

## Management

Management of the institute is vested by the
tract in a board of trustees of twenty members, fi
of whom are to be elected by the members of th
stitute as in the past and five to be appointed by
mayor as representatives of the city. This arra
ment is to exist until the ten years have expired
which such changes in representation shall be mac
are deemed expedient. The large membership of
board of directors is provided to sustain the
terest and support of the present members. It is
provided that the finance committee, which is to
rect the expenditure of the city's appropriation is
composed by two persons named by the presiden
the common council of the city and three member
the board of trustees of the institute. There are t
standing committees under the executive comm
and eleven assisting and advisory committees to
director and the three art committees totaling
one hundred and fifty members.

## anent collection

institutes permanent collection of art treasures
en steadily growing by gifts from friends from
y modest beginning until it now is more than
nt to fill the entire building and is under an ince valuation exceeding $150,000. There have
ix donors whose gifts have been of sufficient pro-
ns to have their names placed in the list of
is of the institution by the board of trustees.

ong the important gifts of the past year were
ertrude N. Schuchardt collection of fifty-five
gs, and sculpture by the late Maxmilian Hoff-
and paintings by prominent Americans, added to
uckner collection.

permanent collection is shown from time to
n various parts of the building at the discretion
exhibition committee and as the space permits.

## uragement of Wisconsin artists

art instiute medal was instituted in 1917 for the
se of encouraging Wisconsin production in fine
Prizes and honorable mentions in the applied
ave also been established and encouragement is
in the applied arts with programs in music,
, drama, pantomime and dance.

of the most important activities of the institute
holding of temporary exhibitions of works of art
ing to institutions, artists and collections from
rts of the United States. These exhibits are con-

## Educational work with adults

A great variety of educational work in art
being carried on constantly through class
lectures. Among them are a business men's
class, a women's sketch class, a class of pictor
spective, a women's painting class, classes in
preciation and the enjoyment of etching and cl
drawing for juveniles. Two lectures a month
en by outside lecturers, and there is a yearl
of thirty lectures on the history of art. Other
include lectures on gardens and home decoratio
ing 1922, sixty-six organizations and clubs
ing thirty-seven hundred adults were enterta
the institute, and sixty-one free lectures were
thirty-six hundred adults.

## Educational work with children

Realizing that the development of the app
of art should begin in childhood, the institute e
to include this appreciation by a wide contact
school children of the city. Over sixteen t
school chilrren visited the institute during
year and over eighteen thousand attended lec
their schools at which the director of the institu
upon art topics. Seventy-one sessions of S
morning and noon drawing calsses were atte
nine thousand children. The pupils of these
are members of the seventh, eighth and hig
grades selected by the principals of the city'
schools.

| Alterations | | Apartments | | | Stores | | Stores and Flats | | | Duplex F | |
|---|---|---|---|---|---|---|---|---|---|---|---|
| No. | Cost | No. | Apts. | Cost | No. | Cost | No. | Apts. | Cost | No. | Co |
| 38 | 159,200 | 1 | 4 | 9,000 | 3 | 13,900 | -- | --- | ----- | 8 | 50 |
| 70 | 57,361 | 1 | 46 | 48,000 | 1 | 2,200 | 3 | 4 | 26,000 | 9 | 69 |
| 214 | 338,653 | 2 | 15 | 36,000 | 7 | 44,310 | 5 | 5 | 54,000 | 40 | 308 |
| 307 | 276,666 | 5 | 83 | 266,500 | 14 | 192,550 | 8 | 8 | 75,000 | 101 | 757 |
| 340 | 216,384 | 2 | 44 | 243,000 | 8 | 76,320 | 13 | 20 | 181,000 | 78 | 614 |
| 238 | 196,214 | 1 | 12 | 75,000 | 8 | 241,500 | 7 | 11 | 77,000 | 58 | 426 |
| 196 | 254,063 | -- | --- | ------ | 8 | 43,950 | 6 | 6 | 54,000 | 61 | 465 |
| 207 | 276,920 | 2 | 46 | 123,000 | 7 | 103,750 | 9 | 12 | 134,200 | 55 | 393 |
| 169 | 179,020 | 2 | 94 | 200,000 | 10 | 123,800 | 5 | 7 | 55,000 | 65 | 457 |
| 181 | 269,632 | 6 | 58 | 351,000 | 10 | 63,200 | 10 | 17 | 151,200 | 55 | 426 |
| 106 | 150,455 | 2 | 56 | 140,000 | 7 | 115,200 | 6 | 8 | 66,500 | 63 | 514 |
| 40 | 163,830 | 1 | 33 | 82,000 | 4 | 29,700 | 6 | 10 | 65,000 | 23 | 174 |
| 2,106 | 2,538,398 | 25 | 491 | 1,573,500 | 87 | 1,050,380 | 78 | 108 | 938,900 | 616 | 4,663 |

| Dwellings | | Garages | | Miscellaneous | | Churches | | Schools | |
|---|---|---|---|---|---|---|---|---|---|
| No. | Cost | No. | Cost | No. | Cost | No. | Cost | No. | Co |
| 20 | 102,500 | 36 | 42,152 | 14 | 2,815 | 1 | 100,000 | -- | -- |
| 22 | 99,150 | 42 | 17,256 | 14 | 2,327 | -- | ------ | -- | -- |
| 117 | 664,500 | 230 | 112,068 | 44 | 15,130 | 1 | 55,000 | -- | -- |
| 134 | 768,915 | 456 | 177,345 | 46 | 16,915 | -- | ------ | 1 | 15 |
| 151 | 775,190 | 440 | 216,510 | 63 | 27,405 | -- | ------ | 1 | 60 |
| 127 | 653,093 | 296 | 142,845 | 42 | 8,296 | 1 | 29,000 | 1 | 115 |
| 95 | 456,700 | 220 | 276,206 | 27 | 5,908 | 1 | 40,000 | -- | -- |
| 123 | 543,850 | 250 | 141,106 | 39 | 11,447 | 2 | 42,200 | -- | -- |
| 87 | 479,050 | 278 | 183,654 | 41 | 21,420 | 1 | 45,000 | -- | -- |
| 104 | 554,850 | 321 | 158,517 | 34 | 12,930 | -- | ------ | -- | -- |
| 96 | 509,125 | 198 | 108,426 | 30 | 17,250 | 1 | 175,000 | -- | -- |
| 54 | 266,600 | 72 | 38,247 | 10 | 5,450 | -- | ------ | -- | -- |
| 1,130 | 5,873,523 | 2,839 | 1,614,332 | 404 | 147,293 | 8 | 486,200 | 3 | 190 |

| Theaters and Halls | | Hospitals | | Factories and Shops | | Office Buildings | | Warehouses | |
|---|---|---|---|---|---|---|---|---|---|
| No. | Cost | No. | Cost | Nos. | Cost | No. | Cost | No. | Co |
| ------ | ------ | -- | ------- | 3 | 2,007,000 | -- | ------ | 2 | 82,5 |
| ------ | ------ | -- | ------- | 1 | 25,000 | 4 | 5,050 | 1 | 6 |
| ------ | ------ | -- | ------- | 6 | 183,300 | 3 | 3,200 | 5 | 31,0 |
| ------ | ------ | -- | ------- | 5 | 90,350 | 4 | 19,400 | 6 | 349,5 |
| ------ | ------ | -- | ------- | 2 | 18,500 | 1 | 1,000 | 4 | 18,2 |
| ------ | ------ | -- | 250,000 | 4 | 88,500 | 1 | 200 | 2 | 1, |

| FIREPROOF CON-STRUCTION | | | MILL CONSTRUCTION | | | ORDINARY CON-STRUCTION | | | VENEER O | |
|---|---|---|---|---|---|---|---|---|---|---|
| No. of Permits | Estimated Cost | Fees | No. of Permits | Estimated Cost | Fees | No. of Permits | Estimated Cost | Fees | No. of Permits | Estim Co |
| 32 | $ 415,399 | $ 540.59 | | | | 25 | $ 407,525 | $ 531.91 | 20 | $ 8 |
| 24 | 408,420 | 532.70 | | | | 12 | 49,300 | 99.38 | 6 | 2 |
| 26 | 1,559,598 | 2,650.71 | | | | 7 | 301,850 | 299.29 | 1 | |
| 46 | 1,833,241 | 2,773.04 | | | | 13 | 229,100 | 275.31 | 12 | 5 |
| 34 | 1,845,693 | 387.83 | 1 | 58,000 | 142.22 | 19 | 98,495 | 255.54 | 17 | 1 |
| 41 | 44,260 | 153.27 | | | | 16 | 104,400 | 225.73 | 17 | 1 |
| 27 | 10,368 | 82.00 | | | | 24 | 69,110 | 122.09 | 95 | 68 |
| 16 | 46,849 | 93.39 | | | | 15 | 51,125 | 126.50 | 53 | 54 |
| 32 | 51,375 | 176.64 | | | | 17 | 221,600 | 251.96 | 27 | 24 |
| 19 | 18,392 | 88.96 | | | | 8 | 13,200 | 34.70 | 33 | 19 |
| 23 | 11,343 | 87.57 | | | | 16 | 39,705 | 76.71 | 182 | 460 |
| 20 | 12,897 | 76.96 | | | | 19 | 43,500 | 95.58 | 27 | 11 |
| 20 | 13,859 | 89.00 | | | | 40 | 118,175 | 260.82 | 66 | 94 |
| 10 | 9,015 | 46.59 | | | | 23 | 111,740 | 193.81 | 191 | 519 |
| 22 | 10,090 | 69.06 | | | | 27 | 131,950 | 249.76 | 126 | 390 |
| 21 | 156,031 | 207.70 | | | | 10 | 184,500 | 192.45 | 46 | 74 |
| 17 | 22,954 | 95.54 | | | | 32 | 82,675 | 155.21 | 204 | 508 |
| 31 | 17,622 | 115.00 | | | | 23 | 132,350 | 184.03 | 235 | 1,176 |
| 29 | 13,737 | 116.00 | | | | 41 | 125,725 | 251.80 | 261 | 966 |
| 35 | 188,208 | 342.38 | | | | 60 | 252,150 | 486.90 | 660 | 2,020 |
| 31 | 183,613 | 375.59 | 2 | 312,000 | 589.46 | 56 | 219,125 | 364.69 | 189 | 500 |
| 42 | 243,694 | 476.34 | | | | 69 | 488,255 | 737.06 | 546 | 1,867 |
| 46 | 30,011 | 174.26 | | | | 37 | 263,762 | 333.04 | 157 | 440 |
| 8 | 6,769 | 44.18 | | | | 32 | 102,125 | 191.74 | 169 | 370 |
| 34 | 12,309 | 119.00 | | | | 39 | 133,200 | 214.75 | 446 | 1,346 |
| 693 | $7,165,747 | $9,914.30 | 3 | $ 370,000 | $ 731.68 | 680 | $3,974,642 | $6,210.76 | 3,786 | 11,106 |

| FIREPROOF CON-STRUCTION | | | MILL CONSTRUCTION | | | ORDINARY CON-STRUCTION | | | VENEER O | |
|---|---|---|---|---|---|---|---|---|---|---|
| No. of Permits | Estimated Cost | Fees | No. of Permits | Estimated Cost | Fees | No. of Permits | Estimated Cost | Fees | No. of Permits | Estim Co |
| 15 | $2,101,760 | $1,404.22 | | | | 7 | $ 124,200 | $ 153.95 | 54 | $ 167 |
| 18 | 36,000 | 148.32 | | | | 12 | 81,600 | 112.42 | 62 | 177 |
| 61 | 183,719 | 428.88 | | | | 55 | 299,220 | 657.18 | 318 | 999 |
| 91 | 575,020 | 956.17 | | | | 95 | 431,195 | 716.57 | 578 | 1,688 |
| 102 | 285,590 | 621.03 | | | | 83 | 474,180 | 700.35 | 563 | 1,442 |
| 84 | 700,427 | 915.70 | 1 | 12,000 | 24.46 | 67 | 340,705 | 584.80 | 374 | 1,094 |
| 50 | 1,228,415 | 1,759.36 | | | | 62 | 201,875 | 380.93 | 317 | 988 |
| 66 | 239,541 | 472.67 | | | | 63 | 452,075 | 607.84 | 352 | 962 |
| 45 | 175,012 | 287.81 | 1 | 300,000 | 565.00 | 76 | 423,600 | 666.75 | 358 | 956 |
| 79 | 218,022 | 448.16 | | | | 87 | 620,877 | 877.57 | 383 | 1,104 |
| 58 | 402,743 | 629.05 | 1 | 58,000 | 142.22 | 51 | 323,250 | 507.42 | 300 | 1,054 |
| 24 | 1,019,492 | 1,842.92 | | | | 22 | 201,865 | 244.98 | 127 | 468 |

| ...ONS AND ...ATIONS | | MOVING | | | WRECKING | | | Total | | |
|---|---|---|---|---|---|---|---|---|---|---|
| ...nated ...ost | Fees | No. of Permits | Estimated Cost | Fees | No. of Permits | Estimated Cost | Fees | No. of Permits | Estimated Cost | Fees |
| 1,170 | $ 148.73 | 4 | $ 4,585 | $ 15.22 | 4 | $ 250 | $ 9.20 | 137 | $ 969,035 | $1,358.6 |
| 4,655 | 198.15 | 1 | 600 | 2.00 | 7 | 1,375 | 17.00 | 117 | 547,248 | 885.0 |
| 0,935 | 188.94 | 1 | 1,200 | 4.00 | 16 | 6,550 | 51.87 | 94 | 1,960,183 | 3,197.8 |
| 1,279 | 580.03 | ----- | ----- | ----- | 10 | 5,025 | 51.01 | 167 | 2,374,310 | 3,792.9 |
| 4,315 | 158.87 | ----- | ----- | ----- | 3 | 250 | 5.66 | 135 | 2,071,888 | 1,049.0 |
| 7,060 | 198.28 | ----- | ----- | ----- | 4 | 325 | 12.65 | 149 | 224,585 | 652.0 |
| 8,975 | 244.15 | ----- | ----- | ----- | 1 | 100 | 3.20 | 251 | 217,378 | 764.6 |
| 2,576 | 395.07 | 1 | 2,000 | 5.00 | 5 | 1,225 | 15.20 | 215 | 298,427 | 825.1 |
| 6,669 | 209.68 | 2 | 1,800 | 7.00 | 4 | 375 | 10.00 | 160 | 366,214 | 743.9 |
| 1,420 | 241.72 | 1 | 1,000 | 4.00 | ----- | ----- | ----- | 141 | 143,793 | 475.1 |
| 2,886 | 252.02 | 4 | 3,000 | 13.00 | 1 | 25 | 2.00 | 318 | 607,084 | 1,284.5 |
| 1,893 | 558.30 | 1 | 300 | 3.00 | 5 | 360 | 16.38 | 145 | 350,113 | 835.4 |
| 5,250 | 349.77 | 3 | 5,800 | 9.00 | 2 | 80 | 3.58 | 251 | 347,318 | 965.0 |
| 4,335 | 234.24 | 7 | 7,000 | 24.00 | 1 | 25 | 1.00 | 322 | 741,195 | 1,403.2 |
| 3,785 | 105.88 | ----- | ----- | ----- | | | | 218 | 566,370 | 1,062.6 |
| 1,365 | 48.00 | 1 | 1,000 | 3.00 | 3 | 260 | 6.24 | 104 | 427,465 | 637.4 |
| 6,766 | 275.19 | 1 | 1,000 | 4.00 | 2 | 105 | 4.25 | 361 | 701,515 | 1,454.4 |
| 5,800 | 219.64 | ----- | ----- | ----- | 1 | 75 | 2.00 | 340 | 1,462,310 | 2,092.0 |
| 3,457 | 261.16 | 2 | 2,600 | 8.00 | | | | 417 | 1,182,229 | 2,067.3 |
| 2,915 | 297.02 | 10 | 8,050 | 38.03 | 1 | 350 | 2.21 | 891 | 2,542,639 | 4,463.8 |
| 7,446 | 329.16 | 5 | 3,950 | 19.20 | 1 | 100 | 3.20 | 404 | 1,346,877 | 2,574.6 |
| 5,462 | 417.66 | 2 | 1,200 | 6.00 | 1 | 50 | 2.00 | 775 | 2,865,971 | 4,548.8 |
| 7,840 | 218.68 | 4 | 2,700 | 12.00 | 2 | 710 | 9.40 | 331 | 815,683 | 1,504.0 |
| 1,570 | 183.79 | 3 | 2,500 | 12.18 | ----- | ----- | ----- | 296 | 532,994 | 1,175.2 |
| 8,124 | 291.60 | 7 | 6,900 | 22.00 | 1 | 110 | 2.00 | 662 | 1,566,756 | 2,852.7 |
| 7,948 | $6,600.73 | 60 | $ 57,185 | $ 210.63 | 75 | $ 17,725 | $ 230.15 | 7710 | 25,229,580 | 42,665.8 |

EACH MONTH—1922

| ...ONS AND ...ATIONS | | MOVING | | | WRECKING | | | Total | | |
|---|---|---|---|---|---|---|---|---|---|---|
| ...nated ...ost | Fees | No. of Permits | Estimated Cost | Fees | No. of Permits | Estimated Cost | Fees | No. of Permits | Estimated Cost | Fees |
| 9,200 | $ 327.68 | 1 | $ 1,200 | $ 4.00 | 9 | $ 1,360 | $ 25.06 | 124 | $2,555,267 | $2,191.0 |
| 7,361 | 187.51 | 2 | 800 | 7.00 | 6 | 505 | 11.00 | 170 | 354,194 | 778.0 |
| 8,653 | 646.72 | 12 | 10,385 | 39.20 | 10 | 1,075 | 27.44 | 670 | 1,832,661 | 3,429.0 |
| 4,166 | 797.70 | 4 | 4,800 | 13.00 | 8 | 1,050 | 15.20 | 1,082 | 2,974,306 | 5,411.1 |
| 4,784 | 889.61 | 5 | 4,700 | 17.00 | 10 | 5,950 | 52.15 | 1,101 | 2,427,894 | 4,886.8 |
| 7,264 | 616.14 | 5 | 3,100 | 16.00 | 8 | 875 | 18.00 | 775 | 2,349,023 | 4,006.1 |
| 5,813 | 720.57 | 5 | 4,300 | 17.00 | 4 | 785 | 11.38 | 638 | 2,679,502 | 4,521.6 |
| 6,620 | 592.61 | 8 | 8,600 | 27.18 | 3 | 1,150 | 12.20 | 697 | 1,930,944 | 3,428.3 |
| 9,120 | 473.35 | 10 | 9,350 | 40.03 | 5 | 350 | 10.30 | 665 | 2,054,084 | 3,748.6 |
| 0,832 | 627.55 | 7 | 9,350 | 28.22 | 4 | 250 | 8.45 | 742 | 2,223,769 | 3,862.4 |
| 9,455 | 391.72 | ----- | ----- | ----- | 4 | 1,125 | 19.37 | 519 | 1,989,269 | 3,272.1 |
| 4,680 | 329.57 | 1 | 600 | 2.00 | 4 | 3,250 | 19.50 | 218 | 1,858,667 | 3,130.3 |

| | No. of Permits | Cost of Work | Inspec-tions | of Fees | Inspec-tions | | Inspec-tions | Inspection | New | Re-modeled |
|---|---|---|---|---|---|---|---|---|---|---|
| uary | 967 | $ 129,521 | 1,629 | $ 2,121.50 | 1,625 | 229 | 434 | $ 70.00 | $ 90.13 | $ 23.23 |
| ruary | 1,139 | 157,530 | 1,487 | 2,282.85 | 1,804 | 188 | 425 | 112.00 | ------- | 10.00 |
| ch | 1,502 | 237,404 | 2,031 | 3,195.25 | 2,716 | 225 | 495 | 108.00 | 37.50 | 5.68 |
| il | 1,622 | 222,735 | 1,955 | 3,471.00 | 2,438 | 92 | 426 | 46.00 | 59.08 | 6.00 |
| y | 2,021 | 274,796 | 2,346 | 4,362.65 | 3,120 | Schools | 482 | 158.00 | 12.50 | 10.00 |
| e | 1,883 | 224,905 | 2,384 | 4,047.30 | 2,813 | 127 | 529 | 228.00 | 138.75 | 15.00 |
| y | 1,592 | 185,621 | 2,018 | 3,523.10 | 2,611 | 222 | 561 | 84.00 | 70.50 | 10.00 |
| gust | 1,720 | 223,612 | 2,264 | 3,757.60 | 2,954 | 111 | 494 | 124.00 | 124.66 | 5.00 |
| tember | 1,944 | 239,182 | 2,365 | 3,993.55 | 2,335 | 205 | 540 | 160.00 | 86.75 | ------- |
| ober | 2,083 | 276,773 | 2,767 | 4,384.20 | 2,730 | 221 | 776 | 156.00 | 134.15 | 5.00 |
| ember | 1,822 | 244,575 | 2,625 | 3,706.10 | 3,434 | 219 | 600 | 188.00 | 193.64 | 17.00 |
| ember | 1,555 | 188,306 | 2,621 | 3,166.80 | 2,773 | 233 | 579 | 218.00 | 5.00 | 5.00 |
| TAL | 19,850 | $2,604,960 | 26,492 | $42,011.90 | 31,354 | 2,072 | 6,341 | $1,652.00 | $952.66 | $111.91 |
| al 1921 | 17,057 | $2,820,446 | 23,311 | $33,500.88 | 28,479 | 2,195 | | | | |

| | Heating | | | | Plastering | | | | Billboards and Sig |
|---|---|---|---|---|---|---|---|---|---|---|---|
| o. f mits | No. of Inspec-tions | Estimated Cost of Work | Fees | No. of Permits | No. of Inspec-tions | Estimated Cost | Fees | No. of Permits | No. of Permits | Estimated Cost | |
| 80 | 167 | $ 100,118 | $ 374 | 439 | 116 | $ 108,735 | $ 402.69 | 298 | 155 | $ 7,578 | |
| 17 | 105 | 66,870 | 256 | 441 | 87 | 68,844 | 297.40 | 266 | 139 | 10,218 | |
| 50 | 134 | 58,096 | 316 | 624 | 107 | 57,356 | 321.12 | 389 | 190 | 40,519 | |
| 51 | 164 | 169,392 | 374 | 554 | 96 | 52,055 | 285.62 | 334 | 236 | 14,422 | |
| 92 | 300 | 169,520 | 708 | 636 | 216 | 130,490 | 626.84 | 309 | 405 | 16,104 | |
| 83 | 377 | 206,782 | 876 | 595 | 206 | 106,606 | 663.04 | 250 | 225 | 11,800 | |
| 42 | 330 | 168,570 | 804 | 582 | 243 | 133,802 | 809.54 | 270 | 219 | 10,471 | |
| 32 | 393 | 167,779 | 944 | 424 | 216 | 129,303 | 773.45 | 251 | 594 | 19,722 | |
| 77 | 421 | 232,530 | 984 | 505 | 196 | 105,566 | 663.52 | 719 | 321 | 17,139 | |
| 60 | 392 | 208,554 | 928 | 698 | 241 | 137,785 | 820.08 | 647 | 453 | 17,499 | |
| 18 | 391 | 147,233 | 898 | 638 | 132 | 127,921 | 649.97 | 426 | 201 | 16,716 | |
| 01 | 204 | 86,624 | 508 | 547 | 119 | 80,231 | 470.33 | 243 | 262 | 15,795 | |
| 03 | 3,378 | $1,782,068 | $7,970 | 6,683 | 1,975 | $1,238,694 | $6,783.60 | 4,402 | 3,400 | $ 197,983 | |

TOTAL COST OF ALL WORK DONE UNDER PERMITS AND NUMBER OF PERMITS I
DURING 1922 AND 1921

| | 1922 | | 1921 |
|---|---|---|---|
| | No. of Permits | Estimated Cost | No. of Permits |
| lding construction | 7,710 | $25,229,580 | 6,814 |
| ctric | 19,850 | 2,604,960 | 17,057 |
| upancy | 309 | ---------- | 1,529 |
| w elevators | 70 | 216,317 | 65 |
| nodeled elevators | 25 | 18,043 | 25 |
| boards and signs | 2,255 | 101,389 | 1,874 |
| n maintenance | 299 | ---------- | 283 |
| board maintenance | 314 | ---------- | 131 |
| tallation of tanks | 270 | 83,328 | 185 |
| nings | 182 | 10,576 | 172 |
| nd pipes, special privilege | 80 | 2,690 | 135 |

| | | | | | | | | |
|---|---|---|---|---|---|---|---|---|
| s _____ | 2 | 226,000 | 19 | 1,260,000 | -------- | ---------- | 4 | 8 |
| Apts._____ | -------- | ----------- | 78 | 938,900 | -------- | ---------- | ------ | ----- |
| ts _____ | 1 | 75,000 | 78 | 969,110 | 7 | 6,020 | 1 | |
| | | | | | | | 616 | 4,66 |
| _____ | -------- | ----------- | 7 | 131,500 | -------- | ---------- | 1123 | 5,74 |
| _____ | 158 | 228,344 | 446 | 704,642 | 442 | 119,896 | 1793 | 56 |
| ous _____ | 2 | 4,040 | 17 | 28,545 | 7 | 4,599 | 378 | 11 |
| _____ | | | 7 | 484,000 | -------- | ---------- | 1 | |
| _____ | | | 3 | 190,000 | | | | |
| and halls_____ | 2 | 1,880,000 | 2 | 83,000 | -------- | ---------- | ------ | ----- |
| _____ | | | 1 | 350,000 | | | | |
| and shops_____ | 8 | 2,209,300 | 34 | 985,900 | ---------- | ---------- | 2 | |
| dings _____ | 1 | 50,000 | 28 | 64,500 | -------- | ---------- | ------ | ----- |
| s _____ | 5 | 420,700 | 17 | 60,800 | 4 | 19,500 | 9 | 4 |
| _____ | 202 | 5,383,791 | 915 | 7,365,145 | 485 | 171,118 | 5807 | 12,33 |

# CRIME

COMPARATIVE TABLE OF ARRESTS, 1921 and 1922

| | 1922 | 1921 | Increase | Decr |
|---|---|---|---|---|
| g family _____ | 280 | 239 | 41 | - |
| _____ | 77 | 65 | 12 | - |
| d battery_____ | 620 | 516 | 104 | - |
| th intent to do great bodily harm_____ | 30 | 30 | -- | - |
| th intent to kill_____ | 16 | 13 | 3 | - |
| d robbery_____ | 15 | 26 | -- | 1 |
| _____ | 116 | 222 | -- | 10 |
| concealed weapons_____ | 57 | 58 | -- | - |
| runkard _____ | 55 | 33 | 22 | - |
| g to delinquency of child_____ | 24 | 68 | -- | 4 |
| conduct _____ | 1,247 | 1,425 | -- | 17 |
| ss _____ | 913 | 754 | 159 | - |
| disorderly_____ | 1,485 | 1,269 | 269 | - |
| ent _____ | 65 | 46 | 19 | - |
| ense _____ | 77 | 93 | -- | 1 |
| d fraudulent issue of bank check_____ | 177 | 172 | 5 | - |
| _____ | 208 | 194 | 14 | - |
| _____ | 12 | 16 | -- | - |
| disorderly house_____ | 596 | 568 | 28 | - |
| gambling house_____ | 344 | 290 | 54 | - |
| sorderly house_____ | 168 | 157 | 11 | - |
| ambling house_____ | 42 | 47 | -- | - |
| s bailee_____ | 54 | 43 | 11 | - |
| om person_____ | 22 | 26 | -- | - |
| rand _____ | 275 | 308 | -- | 3 |
| etit _____ | 123 | 148 | -- | 2 |
| _____ | 28 | 25 | 3 | - |
| stolen property_____ | 29 | 74 | -- | 4 |
| riving _____ | 312 | 248 | 64 | - |
| tomobile without owners consent_____ | 32 | 28 | 4 | - |
| g on railroad property_____ | 42 | 119 | -- | 7 |
| _____ | 420 | 438 | -- | 1 |
| utomobile speed ordinance_____ | 1,343 | 1,466 | -- | 12 |
| ealth ordinance _____ | 33 | 31 | 2 | - |
| icense ordinance _____ | 8 | 45 | -- | 3 |
| notorcycle speed ordinance_____ | 75 | 128 | -- | 5 |
| rules of the road ordinance_____ | 4,249 | 3,720 | 529 | - |
| ass | 3,230 | 2,372 | 858 | |

mitted to home of feebleminded_____ 1
harged by court, officers' cases_____ 1
harged by court, warrant cases_____ 932
harged by chief of police_____ 80
harged by jury _____ 29
harged for want of prosecution_____ 81
harged by district attorney _____ 77
harged by city attorney _____ 1
d _____ 12,887
d guilty and sentence suspended_____ 655
ced _____ 47
ed _____ 10
robation _____ 230
ing _____ 738

Returned to the industrial school for boys___
Returned to the industrial school for girls__
Sentenced to county jail _____
Sentenced to house of correction_____
Sentenced to industrial school for boys_____
Sentenced to industrial school for girls_____
Sentenced to reformatory _____
Sentenced to state prison _____
Settled on payment of costs_____
Turned over to authorities of other places__
Turned over to United States authorities____

Total_____

his number 570 failed to pay their fines and were committed to the house of correction.

## WORK OF DETECTIVE BUREAU, 1922

| Charges | Complaints Received | Arrests | Cases Cleared | Value Stolen Goods | Val er |
|---|---|---|---|---|---|
| donment _____ | 3 | 175 | --- | ------ | |
| ction _____ | --- | --- | --- | ------ | |
| ssory after fact_____ | --- | 5 | --- | ------ | |
| sory before fact_____ | --- | 2 | --- | ------ | |
| tery _____ | --- | 39 | --- | ------ | |
| n _____ | 1 | 1 | --- | ------ | |
| ult and battery_____ | 4 | 27 | 4 | --- | |
| ult and robbery_____ | 20 | 11 | 13 | $ 3,470 | |
| ult with intent to do great bodily harm____ | 1 | 13 | 2 | ------ | |
| ult with intent to kill_____ | 11 | 12 | 7 | ------ | |
| ult with intent to rob_____ | 11 | 6 | 4 | ------ | |
| ult with intent to rape_____ | 4 | 10 | 5 | ------ | |
| mpt burglary _____ | 79 | 3 | 8 | ------ | |
| mpt larceny _____ | 5 | --- | --- | ------ | |
| ardy _____ | --- | 1 | --- | ------ | |
| kmail _____ | 2 | 2 | 2 | ------ | |
| my _____ | --- | 2 | --- | ------ | |
| b explosion _____ | 2 | --- | --- | ------ | |
| lary (residence) _____ | 283 | 33 | 52 | 30,034 | |
| lary (stores, etc.)_____ | 376 | 98 | 72 | 29,237 | |
| ying burglar tools_____ | --- | 1 | --- | ------ | |
| ying concealed weapons_____ | --- | 10 | --- | ------ | |
| mon drunkard _____ | --- | 2 | --- | ------ | |
| dence game _____ | 4 | 5 | 2 | 5,380 | |
| ributing to delinquency of child_____ | --- | 5 | --- | ------ | |
| terfeiting _____ | 4 | --- | 1 | 1 | |
| rderly conduct _____ | --- | 106 | --- | ------ | |
| osing of mortgaged property_____ | 8 | 26 | 5 | 373 | |
| kenness _____ | --- | 6 | --- | ------ | |
| k and disorderly_____ | --- | 32 | --- | ------ | |
| ezzlement _____ | 18 | 67 | 16 | 6,901 | |
| ped prisoner _____ | --- | 2 | --- | ------ | |
| rtion _____ | 1 | 4 | --- | ------ | |
| e pretense _____ | --- | 2 | --- | ------ | |
| ery _____ | 541 | 87 | 226 | 18,633 | |
| ication _____ | --- | 17 | --- | ------ | |
| une telling _____ | --- | 1 | --- | ------ | |
| dulent issue of bank check_____ | 281 | 136 | 211 | 10,213 | |
| tive from justice_____ | --- | 196 | --- | ------ | |
| way robbery _____ | 30 | 9 | 13 | 34,692 | |
| e stealing _____ | 3 | --- | 1 | 785 | |

| | | | | | |
|---|---|---|---|---|---|
| use of ill-fame | 1 | 2 | --- | ------ | ------ |
| utomobile | 467 | 71 | 387 | 351,559 | 303,19 |
| s bailee | 27 | 36 | 14 | 2,693 | 1,62 |
| icycles | 450 | 23 | 178 | 12,075 | 4,85 |
| om person | 63 | 31 | 33 | 6,553 | 1,67 |
| rand | 1,261 | 291 | 471 | 110,999 | 48,90 |
| etit | 787 | 133 | 225 | 7,939 | 2,09 |
| ckpocket | 82 | 2 | 62 | 1,776 | 10 |
| rse snatching | 9 | 2 | 2 | 50 | ------ |
| trick | 40 | 9 | 11 | 1,351 | 26 |
| lascivious behavior | --- | 39 | --- | ------ | ------ |
| | --- | 1 | --- | ------ | ------ |
| | --- | 1 | --- | ------ | ------ |
| er | 1 | 2 | 1 | ------ | ------ |
| | 11 | 4 | 8 | ------ | ------ |
| goods under false pretenses | 6 | 11 | 6 | 435 | 27 |
| money under false pretense | 63 | 51 | 39 | 2,670 | 64 |
| | --- | 3 | --- | ------ | ------ |
| d aiming a firearm | --- | 3 | --- | ------ | ------ |
| | 4 | 24 | 3 | ------ | ------ |
| tolen property | 2 | 19 | 2 | 29 | 2 |
| assist officer | --- | --- | --- | ------ | ------ |
| fficer | --- | --- | --- | ------ | ------ |
| | --- | --- | --- | ------ | ------ |
| g | 1 | --- | --- | 250 | ------ |
| | --- | --- | --- | ------ | ------ |
| | 2 | 6 | 2 | ------ | ------ |
| o without owner's consent | 3 | 12 | 4 | 1,000 | 1,00 |
| orcycle without owner's consent | --- | --- | --- | ------ | ------ |
| to kill | 1 | 5 | 1 | ------ | ------ |
| | --- | --- | --- | ------ | ------ |
| | --- | 133 | --- | ------ | ------ |
| ity ordinances | --- | 25 | --- | ------ | ------ |
| Dyer act | --- | 2 | --- | ------ | ------ |
| ederal prohibition law | --- | 8 | --- | ------ | ------ |
| Iann act | --- | 1 | --- | ------ | ------ |
| arcotic law | --- | 1 | --- | ------ | ------ |
| arole | --- | 11 | --- | ------ | ------ |
| ostal law | 2 | 1 | --- | ------ | ------ |
| tate prohibition enforcement law | 67 | 398 | 21 | ------ | ------ |
| raffic ordinances | --- | 21 | --- | ------ | ------ |
| ruction of property | 23 | 2 | 2 | 287 | ------ |
| us | 8 | 14 | 2 | 125 | 12 |
| S. currency | 5 | --- | --- | 52 | ------ |
| | 47 | 15 | 20 | ------ | ------ |
| and advising felony | --- | 3 | --- | ------ | ------ |
| | 379 | 2 | 110 | 48,104 | 24,55 |
| ls | 5,551 | 3,262 | 2,270 | $687,851 | $419,60 |

# CITY, STATE, COUNTY, COUNTY SCHOOLS, SPECIAL ASSESSMENTS, INCOME A
## OCCUPATIONAL TAXES

l estate and personal property tax

| | |
|---|---:|
| City purposes | $15,234,094.00 |
| State purposes | 1,001,712.55 |
| County purposes | 2,998,964.48 |
| County school purposes | 503,766.25 |

Total real estate and personal property tax _____ $1!

cial taxes

| | | |
|---|---:|---:|
| Installments on 1917 street improvement assessments | $ | 83,267.22 |
| Installments on 1918 street improvement assessments | | 71,032.79 |
| Installments on 1919 street improvement assessments | | 80,807.95 |
| Installments on 1920 street improvement assessments | | 84,628.74 |
| Installments on 1921 street improvement assessments | | 213,396.39 |
| Installments on 1922 street improvement assessments | | 157,406.86 |
| Installments on 1921 street resurfacing assessments | | 30,455.40 |
| Installments on 1922 street resurfacing assessments | | 15,986.63 |
| Sidewalk improvement assessments | | 3,137.90 |
| Sidewalk repairs | | 27,788.94 |
| Sewer improvement assessments | | 36,387.28 |
| House drain and water connections | | 71,939.60 |
| Street oiling | | 112,859.52 |
| Removing snow | | 3,968.73 |
| Destruction of noxious weeds | | 7,598.86 |
| Miscellaneous assessments | | |
| Opening and widening streets and alleys | $ 102,913.90 | |
| Special service, street sanitatoion | 14,648.06 | |
| Removing earth | 993.15 | |
| Delinquent water rates, meter repairs, etc. | 1,294.90 | |
| Forestry service | 24,070.04 | |
| Boulevard improvements | 1,825.69 | |
| Reassessments | 893.21 | 146,638.95 |
| Water pipe assessments | | 45,758.79 |

Total special taxes _____

Total real estate, personal property and special taxes_____ $2(

ome tax

| | | |
|---|---:|---:|
| Normal income tax | | |
| Corporation income | 1,406,527.40 | |
| Individual income | 1,611,294.99 | 3,017,822.39 |

Surtax on incomes (corporation and individual)

| | | |
|---|---:|---:|
| Soldiers bonus tax | 77,458.03 | |
| Soldiers educational tax | 335,500.47 | |
| Teachers retirement fund | 350,972.69 | 763,931.19 |

Total income tax—normal and surtax _____

upational tax

| | | |
|---|---:|---:|
| Coal | | 47,101.97 |

## TAX LEVY FOR 1922 FOR ALL CITY PURPOSES

ity purposes_____$3,971,045.00
ewerage fund_____  145,855.00
rovement fund_____   307,600.00
aintenance fund_____    42,050.00
t fund _____  150,000.00

a under 8-mill limit_____$ 4,616,55

sion fund_____          270,00
onstruction fund_____           50,00
boulevard fund—1922_____           817,43
ice fund—1923_____            22,08
und, 1923_____           187,40
rary fund, 1923_____          252,70
ool fund, 1923_____          319,00
intenance fund, 1923_____         3,673,56
struction fund, 1923_____           200,00
air fund, 1923_____           533,60
tension fund, 1923_____           266,80
education fund, 1923_____           761,31
n fund for auditorium bonds maturing in 1923 _____$13,750.00
n fund for interest on auditorium bonds due in 1923_____ 2,950.00     16,70
readjustment fund_____          169,26
t tax fund_____           10,00
t assessment fund for street and sewer improvements _____       10,00
rchase fund_____            5,00
ty tax for bonds maturing in 1923_____         1,684,94
ty tax for interest on bonds due in 1923_____         1,295,42
rage district tax for bonds maturing in 1923_____             6,50
rage district tax for interest on bonds due in 1923 _____         90
erage district tax for bonds maturing in 1923_____            19,00
erage district tax for interest on bonds due 1923 _____          3,94
rage district tax for bonds maturing in 1923_____            35,00
rage district tax for interest on bonds due in 1923 _____         6,96

al tax levy for all city purposes_____$15,234,09

General city purposes—real estate and
personal property _____$7,300,820.08
Street railway tax_____ 510,084.35
Telephone tax _____ 123,267.22
Boat tonnage tax_____ 190.26
Income tax _____ 1,258,938.61
Occupational tax _____ 50,711.21

ises
Meat _____ 2,868.00
Milk _____ 3,199.00
Home work _____ 1,710.00
Cement walk builders_____ 116.00
Amusement shows _____ 2,440.00
Vehicle _____ 5,564.50
Dogs _____ 2.40
Stationary engineer _____ 4,148.00
Liquor _____ 134,025.00
Soft drinks _____ 1,210.00
Miscellaneous _____ 47,056.98

its
Building _____ 110,856.52
Elevator _____ 2,714.57
Electrical _____ 3,610.00
Sewer connections _____ 10,206.00
Use of street—surface _____ 5,632.00
Use of street—excavation _____ 4,736.00
Covered sidewalk openings_____ 7,492.00

ellaneous
Fees—chattel mortgage, tax certifi-
cates, etc. _____ 8,312.80
Redemption fees and penalties_____ 21,219.05
Health department _____ 18,991.56
Natatoriums
Jackson street _____ 2,226.30
Center street _____ 3,122.83
North avenue _____ 2,902.64
Prairie street _____ 3,573.70
Greenfield avenue _____ 3,924.92
Greenbush street _____ 3,576.61
Fifth avenue _____ 3,391.65

Miscellaneous—continued
Bathing beaches
McKinley park _____
South shore _____
Special privilege _____
Markets _____
Scales _____
Interest on deposits_____
Interest on Liberty loan bonds_____
Interest on U. S. certificates of in-
debtedness _____
Interest on extended taxes_____
Interest on city tax certificates_____
Power plant inspection_____
Rental of lands and buildings
Board of public works_____
Public land commission_____
Rental of space in city hall_____
Municipal and district courts_____
Common council _____
Sales of city property_____
County's share municipal and district
courts' expenses _____
Overrun on taxes of 1921_____
Election commission _____
Building codes _____
Municipal garage _____
Sundry receipts _____
Sale of old equipment_____
Sale of scrap_____
Empty cement bags returned_____
Premium on sale of Liberty bonds___
Police fines _____

$10,

Departmental revenue reverting under the
law to general revenue.
Water works, appropriated
by common council_____

Total_____$10.

GENERAL REVENUE FOR 1923 EXPENDITURES

—real estate and personal property

Sinking fund for bonds due in 1923_____ $1,759,193.80
Interest fund on bonds due in 1923_____ 1,310,179.27
Bond purchase and retirement fund_____ 5,000.00
Departments on Cash basis_____ 718,656.00

$ 3,

—incomes _____ 3,

est on installment street improvement assessments _____$ 389,081.38
est on installment bituminous resurfacing assessments _____ 7,121.42

| Departments | Expense | Total charges Incl. reserves | Total Credits | Net Expense |
|---|---|---|---|---|
| ...ncil | $ 12,968.03 | $ 12,968.03 | $ _____ | $ 12,968.( |
|  | 64,985.12 | 64,985.12 | _____ | 64,985.1 |
| ...ey | 16,882.32 | 16,882.32 | _____ | 16,882.: |
|  | 53,596.63 | 53,596.63 | 1,280.18 | 52,316.4 |
| ...al court | 12,316.92 | 12,316.92 | _____ | 12,316.9 |
| ...court | 9,331.06 | 9,331.06 | _____ | 9,331.( |
| ...f courts | 26,213.70 | 26,213.70 | _____ | 26,213.7 |
| ...of the peace | 634.40 | 634.40 | _____ | 634.4 |
| ...f prisoners | 2,533.30 | 2,533.30 | _____ | 2,533.: |
| ...ppeals | 67.31 | 67.31 | _____ | 67.: |
|  | 51,478.20 | 58,602.29 | 5,485.20 | 53,117.( |
| ...rer |  |  |  |  |
| ...office | 31,795.14 | 31,795.14 | _____ | 31,795.1 |
| ...llections | 79,987.86 | 79,987.86 | _____ | · 79,987.& |
| ...sioner |  |  |  |  |
| ...office | 15,417.06 | 15,417.06 | 9.38 | 15,407.( |
| ...nents | 49,987.86 | 49,987.86 | _____ | 49,987.& |
| ...of review | 84.55 | 84.55 | _____ | 84.E |
| ...ll | 9,209.01 | 9,209.01 | _____ | 9,209.( |
| ...commission | 10,677.56 | 10,677.56 | _____ | 10,677.E |
| ...rd of purchases |  |  |  |  |
| ...office | 7,089.00 | 7,089.00 | _____ | 7,089.( |
| ...n of standards | 291.74 | 291.74 | _____ | 291.7 |
| ...n of purchases | 6,640.00 | 6,640.00 | _____ | 6,640.( |
| ...n of service | 7,318.65 | 7,318.65 | _____ | 7,318.( |
| ...use | 9,719.81 | 9,719.81 | _____ | 9,719.£ |
| ...re and police commissioners | 1,429.29 | 1,429.29 | _____ | 1,429.2 |
| ...ment |  |  |  |  |
| ...office | 24,227.66 | 24,389.06 | 200.00 | 24,189.( |
| ...service | 14,360.47 | 14,360.47 | _____ | 14,360.4 |
| ...evention service | 22,171.03 | 22,171.03 | _____ | 22,171.( |
| ...ghting service | 1,329,749.70 | 1,330,471.85 | 1,482.75 | 1,328,989.1 |
| ...shop | 43,331.41 | 43,331.41 | 3,379.02 | 39,952.: |
| ...gs and grounds | 38,621.20 | 38,814.32 | 1,000.74 | 37,813.£ |
| ...ary | 3,038.00 | 3,038.00 | _____ | 3,038.( |
| ...us | 4,365.00 | 4,365.00 | _____ | 4,365.( |
| ...rtment |  |  |  |  |
| ...office | 33,636.04 | 33,636.04 | 930.00 | 32,706.0 |
| ...service | 17,560.00 | 17,560.00 | _____ | 17,560.( |
| ...service | 1,372,435.12 | 1,373,765.12 | 500.00 | 1,373,265.1 |
| ...gs and grounds | 18,425.85 | 18,425.85 | _____ | 18,425.£ |
| ...lice alarm system |  |  |  |  |
| ...office | 5,402.98 | 5,402.98 | _____ | 5,402.9 |
| ...nance and operation | 52,182.38 | 52,182.38 | 1,850.65 | 50,331.7 |
| ...ction | 20,616.40 | 20,616.40 | _____ | 20,616.4 |
| ...eights and measures |  |  |  |  |
| ...ion | 17,964.78 | 17,964.78 | _____ | 17,964.7 |
| ...s | 8,136.50 | 8,136.50 | _____ | 8,136.E |
| ...uilding and elevator inspection |  |  |  |  |
| ...office | 21,247.76 | 21,247.76 | _____ | 21,247.7 |
| ...ion division | 63,568.67 | 63,568.67 | 16.05 | 63,552.( |
| ...xamining of engineers | 7,171.59 | 7,171.59 | _____ | 7,171.E |
| ...rtment |  |  |  |  |
| ...office |  |  |  |  |
| ...ecutive | 24,536.71 | 24,536.71 | 168.37 | 24,368.: |
| ...al statistics | 6,167.03 | 6,167.03 | _____ | 6,167.( |
| ...health |  |  |  |  |
| ...ild welfare division | 7,966.79 | 7,966.79 | _____ | 7,966.7 |
| ...od inspection division | 47,180.56 | 47,180.56 | _____ | 47,180.E |
| ...nitary inspection division | 43,062.11 | 43,062.11 | 67.50 | 42,994.( |

| | | | |
|---|---|---|---|
| Hospitals and sanatoriums | | | |
| South View hospital | 77,701.15 | 77,701.15 | .......... |
| inston Emergency hospital | 52,518.95 | 52,518.95 | .......... |
| reau of smoke suppression | 7,084.74 | 7,084.74 | .......... |
| partment of public works | | | |
| Bureau of street sanitation | | | |
| General office | 16,863.84 | 16,863.84 | .......... |
| Supervision—field | 49,249.52 | 49,249.52 | .......... |
| Street cleaning division | | | |
| Cleaning streets and alleys | 291,846.57 | 292,010.94 | 117.30 |
| Sprinkling service | 45,111.62 | 45,111.62 | 1,100.50 |
| Flushing service | 67,727.90 | 67,727.90 | 299.60 |
| Refuse disposal | | | |
| Ash disposal | 498,030.86 | 498,030.86 | .......... |
| Garbage collection | 272,153.73 | 272,153.73 | 465.00 |
| Dead animal disposal | 2,166.00 | 2,166.00 | .......... |
| Cleaning sewer catch basins | 30,282.11 | 30,282.11 | .......... |
| Ward yards | 27,803.21 | 27,803.21 | 2,845.39 |
| Minor street repairs | 59,672.77 | 59,672.77 | 3,557.65 |
| Miscellaneous service | | | |
| Public drinking fountains | 11,556.46 | 11,956.46 | .......... |
| Skating rinks | 1,297.37 | 1,297.37 | .......... |
| Street signs | 5,117.80 | 5,117.80 | 40.00 |
| Miscellaneous | 7,079.12 | 7,079.12 | .......... |
| Special work—Rotary fund | 64,083.01 | 64,083.01 | 81,155.21 |
| Bureau of plumbing inspection | | | |
| General office | 5,096.80 | 5,096.80 | 10.00 |
| Inspection division | 23,001.35 | 23,001.35 | .......... |
| Bureau of sewers | | | |
| General office | 14,934.18 | 14,934.18 | .......... |
| Store-yards | 10,539.25 | 10,539.25 | .......... |
| Sewers | | | |
| Cleaning and flushing division | 53,339.74 | 53,339.74 | 1,516.62 |
| Repairs division | 29,029.34 | 29,029.34 | 2,054.20 |
| Special work—Rotary fund | 16,132.57 | 16,132.57 | 16,632.38 |
| Commissioner | | | |
| General office | 15,543.72 | 15,543.72 | 12.50 |
| Audits and accounts | 10,495.31 | 10,495.31 | .......... |
| Special assessments | 9,676.52 | 9,676.52 | .......... |
| Bureau of bridges and public buildings | | | |
| General office | 15,742.47 | 15,742.47 | .27 |
| Bridges and viaducts | | | |
| Superintendence | 5,627.82 | 5,627.82 | .......... |
| Operation | 204,396.44 | 204,396.44 | 2,786.82 |
| Maintenance and repairs | 162,105.20 | 162,105.20 | 44,066.79 |
| City hall | | | |
| Heat and power division | 45,292.38 | 45,292.38 | 762.19 |
| Electrical service | 11,152.39 | 11,152.39 | 3,316.17 |
| Janitorial service | 33,556.36 | 33,556.36 | 346.12 |
| Elevator service | 9,955.17 | 9,955.17 | .......... |
| Telephone service | 16,426.30 | 16,426.30 | 1,533.62 |
| General service | 10,416.53 | 10,505.03 | 1,409.91 |
| Natatoriums | 92,002.26 | 92,002.26 | 196.40 |
| Bathing beaches | 17,150.75 | 19,121.12 | 16.40 |
| Municipal Garage | 63,332.69 | 63,332.69 | 20,901.48 |
| Public comfort stations | 919.24 | 919.24 | .......... |
| Special work—Rotary fund | 29,002.73 | 29,002.73 | 32,070.98 |
| Construction | 24,289.11 | 24,302.06 | 11,214.85 |
| Bureau of engineers | | | |
| General office | 8,785.54 | 8,785.54 | 2,472.22 |
| Engineering division | 74,399.55 | 74,399.55 | 12,729.05 |
| Bureau of street construction and repairs | | | |
| General office | 12,392.46 | 12,392.46 | .......... |

| | | | | |
|---|---|---|---|---|
| Amounts forwarded | $6,839,551.55 | $6,857,081.53 | $319,973.16 | $6,537,108 |
| of power plants | | | | |
| cinerator power plant | 8,331.37 | 8,331.37 | | 8,331. |
| cinerator | 147,564.35 | 147,564.35 | | 147,564. |
| ushing stations | | | | |
| Jones Island plant | 48,413.29 | 48,413.29 | 23,083.92 | 25,329. |
| Kinnickinnic river plant | 30,793.09 | 30,793.09 | | 30,793. |
| Milwaukee river plant | 14,662.87 | 14,662.87 | 37.62 | 14,625. |
| cKinley park | 4,709.42 | 4,709.42 | | 4,709. |
| of illumination service | | | | |
| neral office | 16,906.71 | 17,284.46 | | 17,284. |
| boratory | 3,219.49 | 3,219.49 | 30.50 | 3,188. |
| orehouse | 8,065.00 | 8,065.00 | | 8,065. |
| reet lighting | | | | |
| Operation | 147,253.22 | 147,253.22 | 1,314.08 | 145,939. |
| Maintenance | 117,811.51 | 124,467.67 | 324.45 | 124,143. |
| nstruction | 10,301.23 | 10,301.23 | 3,544.30 | 6,756. |
| iscellaneous | 4,273.94 | 4,586.44 | 191.52 | 4,394. |
| lection commissioners | | | | |
| l office | 12,999.54 | 12,999.54 | 3,060.00 | 9,939. |
| ns | | | | |
| ring primary | 30,804.74 | 30,804.74 | | 30,804. |
| ring election | 21,086.45 | 21,086.45 | | 21,086. |
| ll primary | 21,061.85 | 21,061.85 | | 21,061. |
| ll election | 18,984.65 | 18,984.65 | | 18,984. |
| | 12,790.48 | 12,790.48 | | 12,790. |
| arbor commissioners | | | | |
| l office | 6,807.46 | 6,807.46 | | 6,807. |
| ering | 1,322.38 | 1,322.38 | | 1,322. |
| us | | | | |
| n council—Contingent | 49,660.50 | 57,340.03 | 10,283.43 | 47,056. |
| n council—Special | 156,772.87 | 195,818.43 | 52,863.31 | 142,955. |
| ttorney—Workmen's compensation | 34,841.96 | 34,841.96 | 132.80 | 34,709. |
| TOTAL | $7,768,989.92 | $7,840,591.40 | $414,839.09 | $7,425,752. |
| ance | | | | |

| | Reserves of 1921 | Taxes | Revenue 1921 Surplus | Total Revenue | Charges against Revenue | Expense | Balance | Reserves |
|---|---|---|---|---|---|---|---|---|
| | $ 95,859.36 | $3,540,000.00 | $1,620,808.44 | $ 5,256,667.80 | $ | $4,710,680.74 | $545,987.06 | $131,026.95 |
| | 773.02 | 410,000.00 | 51,148.13 | 461,921.15 | | 460,781.11 | 1,140.04 | 123.00 |
| | 11,044.85 | 294,000.00 | 23,896.57 | 328,941.42 | | 269,602.44 | 59,338.98 | 18,563.98 |
| | 44,299.49 | 270,000.00 | 24,936.88 | 339,236.37 | | 237,811.60 | 101,424.77 | 63,518.35 |
| education | 11,094.11 | 1,012,500.00 | 733,740.17 | 1,757,334.28 | | 540,844.99 | 196,118.23 | 55,525.00 |
| to capital account | | | | | 913,908.56 | | | |
| sinking fund | | | | | 106,462.50 | | | |
| | 2,504.64 | 187,405.25 | 24,667.00 | 213,976.89 | 10,706.25 | 195,959.37 | 7,311.27 | 7,293.84 |
| | | | 571.47 | 571.47 | | 32.00 | 539.47 | |
| | 12,735.78 | 218,425.75 | 78,583.41 | 309,744.94 | 2,208.75 | 267,589.09 | 39,947.10 | 25,886.00 |
| ission | | 22,336.00 | 3,581.81 | 25,917.81 | | 23,720.57 | 2,197.24 | |
| | 157,829.96 | | 1,207,718.37 | 1,365,548.33 | | 1,222,178.19 | *576,480.64 | 38,867.12 |
| to general revenue | | | | | 225,000.00 | | | |
| to capital account | | | | | 321,483.97 | | | |
| to sinking fund | | | | | 22,087.50 | | | |
| to special and trust | | | | | | | | |
| t | | | | | 151,279.31 | | | |
| ulevard fund | 2,964.24 | 544,958.53 | 38,062.62 | 585,985.39 | | 585,985.39 | | |
| | | 68,119.82 | 417.00* | 67,702.82 | | 64,883.01 | 2,819.81 | |
| d | | 21,000.00 | 2,137.74* | 18,862.26 | | 19,362.26 | *500.00 | |
| drive | | 204,359.44 | | 204,359.44 | 204,359.44 | | | |
| rive—maintenance | | | 6,545.30 | 6,545.30 | | 6,545.30 | | |
| | $339,105.45 | $6,793,104.79 | $3,811,105.43 | $10,943,315.67 | $1,957,496.28 | $8,605,976.06 | $379,843.33 | $340,814.24 |

## DEPARTMENTAL REVENUE FROM TAXES FOR 1923

| | |
|---|---|
| Schhool operation | $3,673,568.02 |
| School repairs | 533,600.00 |
| School trades | 319,000.00 |
| School extension | 266,800.00 |
| Board of industrial education | 761,316.44 |
| Public museum | 187,400.00 |
| Public library | 252,700.00 |
| City service commission | 22,081.00 |
| Total | $6,016,465.46 |

| | Balance carried over from 1921 | Bond Proceeds | Taxes and Revenues | Total for for Improvements | Cost of Improvements for 1922 | Transferred to General Acct. Revenue | Balance | Reserves for Contracts and Purchase Orders |
|---|---|---|---|---|---|---|---|---|
| nt | $ 32,542.43 | 200,000.00 | $ 39,160.69 | $ 271,703.12 | $ 253,049.27 | $ | $ 18,652.85 | $ 3,500.00 |
| nts | 234,026.60 | 500,000.00 | 726.23 | 734,752.83 | 144,028.06 | | 590,724.17 | 55,204.75 |
| | 286,530.99 | | | 286,530.99 | 5,917.55 | | 280,613.44 | |
| duct | 37,503.44* | | 84,364.17 | 46,860.73 | 18,641.95 | | 28,218.78 | |
| ge | 249,999.77 | 600,000.00 | | 849,999.77 | | | 849,999.77 | |
| iaduct | 183,917.26 | | | 183,917.26 | | | 183,917.26 | |
| bridge | 4,042.87 | | | 4,042.87 | | | 4,042.87 | |
| ige | | 150,000.00 | | 150,000.00 | | | 150,000.00 | |
| torium | 70,000.00 | | | 70,000.00 | | | 70,000.00 | |
| bridge | 509.61 | | | 509.61 | | | 509.61 | |
| tal | 57,487.55 | | 53,000.00 | 110,487.55 | 1.77 | | 110,485.78 | |
| torium | 319.76 | | | 319.76 | 319.76 | | | |
| shore | 70,000.00 | | | 70,000.00 | | | 70,000.00 | |
| nley park | 50,045.66 | | | 50,045.66 | | | 50,045.66 | |
| n land contracts | | | 220,800.00 | 220,800.00 | 220,800.00 | | | |
| | 272,886.85 | | | 272,886.85 | 8,549.90 | | 264,336.95 | |
| onstruction | 9,939.78 | | | 9,939.78 | | | 9,939.78 | |
| tion | 499,992.36 | | | 499,992.36 | 28,700.00 | | 471,292.36 | |
| olition fund | 220,658.63 | 240,000.00 | | 460,658.63 | 94,087.95 | | 366,570.68 | 141,239.93 |
| construction, sup- | | | 2,576.07 | 2,576.07 | 2,576.07 | | | |
| construction, ex- | 42,262.99 | | | 42,262.99 | 23,132.79 | | 1,130.38 | 1,130.38 |
| gen. acct. revenue | | | | | | 17,999.82 | | |
| nt, construction, amping station | 668,919.36 | | 331,146.72 | 1,000,006.08 | 274,567.60 | | 725,498.48 | 725,498.48 |
| nt, construction, lant | | | 5,761.00 | 5,761.60 | 5,761.00 | | | |
| e fund | 5,660.93 | 350,000.00 | | 355,660.93 | 123,021.23 | | 232,639.70 | |
| | 262,556.07 | | 197,814.14 | 460,370.21 | 231,789.19 | | 228,581.02 | |
| c lighting system | 56,195.96 | | | 56,195.96 | 24,032.77 | | 32,163.19 | |
| truction | 1,997,057.86 | 500,000.00 | 200,049.95 | 2,697,107.81 | 861,652.86 | | 1,835,454.95 | 234,286.28 |
| tion | 1,587,480.86 | | 3,022,379.22 | 4,609,860.08 | 1,508,805.90 | | 3,101,054.18 | 1,923,202.86 |
| l education | 511,440.78 | | 913,908.56 | 1,425,349.34 | 672,697.44 | | 752,651.90 | 147,758.52 |
| | $7,336,970.49 | $2,540,000.00 | $5,071,686.75 | $14,948,658.24 | $4,502,133.66 | $17,999.82 | $10,428,524.76 | $3,231,821.20 |

| | Balance carried over from 1921 | Taxes | Revenue | Total Credits | Expenditures for 1922 |
|---|---|---|---|---|---|
| bonds | $1,961,355.70 | $1,835,693.80 | $193,750.50* | $3,990,800.00 | $1,931,500.00 |
| park land contracts | 100.00 | | | 100.00 | |
| ds | 1,272,894.26 | 1,374,806.77 | 73,387.50** | 2,721,088.53 | 1,301,465.28 |
| l retirement fund | 23,095.53 | 5,000.00 | | 28,095.53 | 8,263.32 |
| | $3,257,445.49 | $3,215,500.57 | $267,138.00 | $6,740,084.06 | $3,241,228.60 |

m on bonds sold—$153,750.50.
interest on bonds sold—$41,250.00.

| | Balance carried over from 1921 | Taxes and Revenue | Local Assessments | Total Credits | Cost of Local Serv. and Impvts. for 1922 | Transferred to Gen. Acct. Surplus | Balance Dec. 31, 1922 | Contract Reserves |
|---|---|---|---|---|---|---|---|---|
| d alleys | $ | $ 150,000.00 | $102,913.90 | $ 252,913.90 | $ 68,052.71 | $184,861.19 | $ | $ |
| permanent | 64,110.00 | 1,295,133.08 | | 1,359,243.08 | 1,317,669.53 | 2,778.55 | 38,795.00 | 38,795.00 |
| bituminous resurfacing | | 129,400.61 | | 129,400.61 | 127,150.06 | 2,250.55 | | |
| | | 55,599.33 | 112,859.52 | 168,458.85 | 140,031.17 | 28,427.68 | | |
| d ice from sidewalks | | | 3,968.73 | 3,968.73 | 3,968.73 | | | |
| weeds | | | 7,598.86 | 7,598.86 | 7,598.86 | | | |
| | | | 993.15 | 993.15 | 993.15 | | | |
| | | | 40.60 | 40.00 | 40.00 | | | |
| ts | 419,365.18 | 302,505.74* | 36,387.28 | 758,258.20 | 315,281.68 | | 442,976.52 | 148,292.51 |
| ater connections | | | 71,939.60 | 71,939.60 | 71,939.60 | | | |
| new mains | 74,185.62 | 151,279.31 | 45,758.79 | 271,223.72 | 244,802.97 | | 26,420.75 | 26,420.75 |
| Biddie, Cedar and Lake | 211,504.94 | 3,100,000.00** | | 3,311,504.94 | 333,645.38 | | 2,977,859.56 | |
| | | 16,402.89 | 27,788.94 | 44,191.83 | 44,191.83 | | | |
| | | | 24,070.04 | 24,070.04 | 24,070.04 | | | |
| ts | | | 1,825.69 | 1,825.69 | 1,825.69 | | | |
| | $769,165.74 | $5,200,320.96 | $436,144.50 | $6,405,631.20 | $2,701,261.40 | $218,317.97 | $3,486,051.83 | $213,508.26 |

0 bond proceeds.
oceeds.

# SUMMARY CONSOLIDATED BALANCE SHEET

As of December 31, 1922.

| | General Account | Capital Account | Sinking Fund | Special and Trust Accounts |
|---|---|---|---|---|
| | $ 3,969,072.69* | $ 7,162,575.93 | $ 424,482.30 | $3,082.876.44 |
| y loan bonds | 500,000.00 | | | |
| cates of indebtedness | 762,500.00 | | | |
| of bank deposits | 100,000.00 | | | |
| e the city | 14,743,173.07 | 675,159.44 | 3,074,373.07 | 4,605,197.33 |
| to be placed on tax roll | | | | 1,993,389.49 |
| | 53,391.13 | | | |
| rized, but not sold | | 2,890,000.00 | | |
| property and equipment | | 69,333,240.00 | | |
| assets | $12,189,991.51 | $71,060,975.37 | $3,498,855.46 | $9,681,463.26 |
| ayable | $ 477,190.82 | $ 299,210.61 | | $ 106,167.07 |
| t | | 27,750,500.00 | | |
| liabilities | $ 477,190.82 | $28,049,710.61 | | $ 106,167.07 |
| nues, Appropriations and Reserves | | | | |
| ssets over liabilities | $11,712,800.69 | $43,011,264.76 | $3,498.855.46 | $9,575,296.19 |
| ions and Reserves | | | | |
| red balances | $ | $ 7,196,703.56 | | $3,272,543.57 |
| r contracts | 39,341.00 | 3,155,516.04 | | 213,508.26 |
| r purchase orders | 15,709.05 | | | |
| r resolution appropriations | 16,110.98 | 76,305.16 | | |
| r miscellaneous obligations | 341,254.69 | | | |
| r delinquent assessment for street and sewer improvements | 50,000.00 | | | |
| r estimated delinquent taxes | 54,907.44 | | | |
| r tax deficits | 119,454.90 | | | |
| r taxation readjustment | 689,304.58 | | | |
| r delinquent income tax | 113,274.83 | | | |
| r street improvement certificates owned by city | 7,895.53 | | | |
| r delinquent accounts receivable | 2,768.32 | | | |
| r stores investment | 26,996.11 | | | |
| r retirement of bonded debt | | | 2,059,300.00 | |
| r interest on bonded debt | | | 1,419,623.25 | |
| r purchase and retirement of bonds | | | 19,832.21 | |
| r retirement of park land contracts | | | 100.00 | |
| r trust relations | | | | 6,089,244.36 |
| authorizations and reserves | $ 1,477,017.44 | $10,428,524.76 | $3,498,855.46 | $9,575,296.19 |
| s and estimated revenues over liabilities, ions and reserves | 10,235,783.25** | 32,582,740.00 | | |

ance.

r 1913 expenditures unappropriated $10,138,777.90 plus surplus $97,005.35.

# GENERAL ACCOUNT BALANCE SHEET

## As of December 31, 1922

| to general account liabilities | | |
|---|---|---|
| r ......................................................... | *$ 3,969,072.69 | |
| bonds................................................ | 500,000.00 | |
| of indebtedness............................. | 762,500.00 | |
| nk deposits....................................... | 100,000.00 | |
| | | |
| e—tax not in arrears. | | |
| levy, real estate and per- | | |
| operty ..................................... | $18,516,586.50 | |
| levy, income............................... | 2,674,260.25 | |
| levy, surtax on income.......... | 626,194.78 | |
| levy, extended........................... | 341,880.37 | |
| | | 22,158,921.90 |
| e, tax in arrears. | | |
| ificates, delinquent tax, real estate. | | |
| ......................................... | $ 138,024.50 | |
| ......................................... | 62,041.09 | |
| ......................................... | 13,776.34 | |
| x, personal property, bank | | |
| | 372,279.52 | |
| x, personal property, chief | | |
| ......................................... | 127,526.00 | |
| x, income............................... | 113,274.83 | |
| vement certificates owned | | |
| ......................................... | 7,895.53 | |
| | | 834,817.81 |
| le, general......................................... | 104,163.20 | |
| le, due from special and trust account..... | 2,965,397.11 | |
| to future expense only. | | |
| ......................................... | 53,391.13 | |
| | | |
| evenue and surplus. | | |
| ue for 1923 ..................................... | 3,074,373.07 | |
| | | |
| revenue for 1923................................... | 10,368.75 | |
| | | |
| eral account assets............................. | $26,294,860.28 | |

Liabilities to be paid out of general account assets.
Warrants payable.

| | |
|---|---|
| General city ......................................... | $144,284.02 |
| School operation .............................. | 21,618.23 |
| School repair ..................................... | 18,047.98 |
| Trade school ...................................... | 6,226.59 |
| Extension school .............................. | 5,962.08 |
| Industrial education ........................ | 182,872.43 |
| Park board, park and boulevard fund... | 59,462.05 |
| Park Board, forestry fund................ | 1,064.12 |
| Park board, zoo fund ....................... | 4,582.50 |
| Public library ..................................... | 11,240.53 |
| Public museum .................................. | 20,098.61 |
| City service commission................... | 734.22 |
| Election commission ....................... | 1,057.46 |

Reserve for delinquent assessments for street and sewer improvements ............................................................
Reserve for estimated delinquent taxes...............................
Reserve for tax deficits ..................................................
Reserve for taxation readjustment .................................

Reserve for delinquent income tax...................................
Reserve for street improvement certificates owned by the city

Reserve for delinquent accounts receivable.....................
Due to other funds.............................................................

Investments.
  Reserved for stores investment.....................................
General account revenue, balances and surplus..

| | |
|---|---|
| General revnue for 1923.......................... | $7,207,054.26 |
| General reserves for 1923....................... | 71,601.48 |
| General surplus for 1923........................ | 57,976.26 |
| | |
| Departmental revenue for 1923............... | $6,016,465.46 |
| Departmental reserves for 1923............. | 340,814.24 |
| Departmental surplus for 1923............... | 39,029.09 |

Total general account liabilities.................. $

## CAPITAL ACCOUNT BALANCE SHEET

### As of December 31, 1922.

|  | | Liabilities. | |
|---|---|---|---|
| treasurer_____ | $7,162,575.93 | Warrants payable. | |
| other funds_____ | 675,159.44 | General city warrants___$148,483.92 | |
| horized, but not sold_____ | 2,890,000.00 | School construction warrants _____ 40,173.80 | |
|  | | Park board, lake shore drive warrants ____ 1,578.41 | |
| t property and equipment. | | Sewerage commission warrants _____ 108,974.48 | |
| _____$12,500,000.00 | | | |
| tures _____ 45,000,000.00 | | | $    299,2 |
| res and equip- | | Liabilities for permanent property and equipment. | |
| nent _____ 2,500,000.00 | | Principal of bonded debt_____ 27,750,5( | |
| orium stock ___ 283,240.00 | | Gifts and requests_____ 8,2 | |
| en Homes Com- | | Surplus-permanent property and equip- | |
| any stock _____ 50,000.00 | | ment (provided for by revenue) 32,574,5( | |
|  | 60,333,240.00 | Reserve for improvements in progress__ 10,428,5: | |
|  | | Total capital account liabilities_$71,060,9' | |
| Total capital account assets___ | $71,060,975.37 | | |


## SINKING FUND BALANCE SHEET

### As of December 31, 1922.

|  | | Liabilities. | |
|---|---|---|---|
|  | | Redemption funds. | |
| treasurer _____$ 81,128.40* | | Bonds _____$2,059,300.00 | |
| anty Trust Co.___ 505,610.79 | | Park land contracts__ 100.00 | |
|  | $  424,482.39 | | $2,059,4( |
| other funds_____ | 3,074,373.07 | Interest funds. | |
|  | | Bonds _____ 1,419,6: | |
|  | | Bond purchase fund_____ 19,8: | |
| Total sinking fund assets_____ | $3,498,855.46 | Total sinking fund liabilities_$3,498,8: | |

lance.

## SPECIAL AND TRUST ACCOUNT BALANCE SHEET

### As of December 31, 1922.

| | | |
|---|---:|---:|
| r | | $3,082,876.44 |
| funds | | 7,370,594.44 |
| ivable in arrears | | |
| tificates | | |
| ssessments for street and provements | | |
| | $ 1,145.34 | |
| | 19,045.54 | |
| l—issued by public works de-ment | 18,421.32 | |
| l—issued by street commis-ers | 77,576.60 | |
| ssessments on street improve-t bonds | 1,504.38 | |
| | | 117,693.18 |
| ivable, to be placed on tax roll. | | |
| on street improvement assessments. | | |
| for 1918, C-1 to C-5183 | $ 66,456.85 | |
| for 1919, D-1 to D-5579 | 149,417.44 | |
| for 1920, E-1 to E-3679 | 229,033.92 | |
| for 1921, F-1 to F-7208 | 755,728.24 | |
| for 1922, G-1 to G-6048 | 928,733.44 | |
| | | 2,129,369.89 |
| bituminous resurfacing assess-ts. | | |
| for 1921, FR-1 to FR-3337 | $107,942.17 | |
| for 1922, GR-1 to GR-1817 | 94,314.32 | |
| | | 202,256.49 |
| special and trust account assets | | $12,802,790.44 |

**Liabilities.**

Warrants payable, general city

Installments on street improvement assessments paid in full.

| | | |
|---|---|---:|
| Assessments for 1918, C-1 to C-5183 | $ | 467.5 |
| Assessments for 1919, D-1 to D-5579 | | 500.8 |
| Assessments for 1920, E-1 to E-3679 | | 2,051.5 |
| Assessments for 1921, F-1 to F-7208 | | 7,043.7 |
| Assessments for 1922, G-1 to G-6048 | | 17,281.2 |

Installments on bituminous resurfacing assessments paid in full.

| | | |
|---|---|---:|
| Assessments for 1921, FR-1 to FR-3337 | $ | 461.3 |
| Assessments for 1922, GR-1 to GR-1817 | | 939.9 |

Accounts payable due to general account

Trust funds

Street and sewer improvement certificates

Street commissioner's certificates

Installments on street improvement bonds placed on tax roll.

Reserve for interest installments on street improvement assessments.

| | | |
|---|---|---:|
| On 1918 street improvement assessments | $ | 3,816.5 |
| On 1919 street improvement assessments | | 12,347.8 |
| On 1920 street improvement assessments | | 24,589.2 |
| On 1921 street improvement assessments | | 98,576.6 |
| On 1922 street improvement assessments | | 141,745.1 |

Reserve for interest installments on bituminous resurfacing assessments.

| | | |
|---|---|---:|
| On 1921 bituminous resurfacing assessments | $ | 14,079.4 |
| On 1922 bituminous resurfacing assessments | | 14,385.9 |

Reserve for local service and improvements in progress

Total special and trust account liabilities

## FOR FUTURE INDEBTEDNESS

### January 1, 1923.

ion Five Per Cent of Average Total Valuation of All Taxable Propery for Five Years Last Past.

| | | | |
|---|---|---|---|
| valuation | $574,020,559.00 | Five per cent of five year average | $31,964,572 |
| valuation | 588,556,266.00 | Bonded debt Jan. 1, 1922 $23,965,500.00 | |
| valuation | 675,611,540.00 | Bonds issued in 1922 3,050,000.00 | |
| valuation | 681,198,160.00 | Bonds authorized, but not | |
| valuation | 677,070,755.00 | sold 2,890,000.00 | |
| | | $29,905,500.00 | |
| rate | $3,196,457,280.00 | Sinking fund for bonds | |
| ear average | 639,291,456.00 | due in 1923 $2,146,800.00 | |
| | | $27,758,700.00 | |
| | | Bonds purchased in 1922 8,200.00 | |

Net bonded debt, Jan. 1, 1923 $27,750,500

Net margin for further bond issues, January 1, 1923 $ 4,214,072

## TOTAL AMOUNTS AND PURPOSES OF BONDS OUTSTANDING

| | | | |
|---|---|---|---|
| ds | $5,993,750.00 | Market | $ 275,000 |
| system | 4,258,000.00 | Bath (natatoria and bathing beaches) | 275,000 |
| ing | 2,375,000.00 | Viaduct | 198,750 |
| | 2,226,500.00 | Waterworks | 150,000 |
| | 2,141,500.00 | West sewerage district | 140,000 |
| ghting system | 1,920,000.00 | Fire department | 107,500 |
| | 1,902,750.00 | South sewerage district | 80,500 |
| harbor improvements | 1,426,200.00 | Historical museum | 60,000 |
| ning | 920,000.00 | Auditorium | 58,750 |
| school | 900,000.00 | Garbage plant | 50,000 |
| sing abolition | 600,000.00 | Public library | 28,500 |
| rovement | 522,000.00 | East sewerage district | 18,000 |
| artment | 499,300.00 | Bath and library | 10,000 |
| | 335,500.00 | Flushing tunnel | 6,000 |
| nd dredging | 322,000.00 | | |

Total $27,750,500

### UE OF MILWAUKEE PROPERTY

| | |
|---|---|
| ssessed by state tax commission | $ 79,860,335 |
| railroads $42,225,000 | |
| railway and light- | |
| companies 27,958,871 | |
| al property 3,133,014 | |
| ne, telegraph and | |
| ing car companies 6,543,450 | |
| ocally assessed | 677,070,755 |
| alue assessed under occupation | |
| 2,224,247 | |

### VALUE OF PROPERTY EXEMPT FROM TAXA
### TION

| | |
|---|---|
| United States government | $ 2,853,0 |
| State of Wisconsin | 1,185,2 |
| County of Milwaukee | 1,211,0 |
| City of Milwaukee | 68,424,4 |
| Churches, parsonages, parochial schools | 13,224,5 |
| Colleges, universities and academies | 3,066,7 |
| Cemeteries | 1,203,5 |
| Lodges and benevolent institutions | 6,661,2 |

| | Street Resurfacing | | Street and Alley Improvements | | | House drains | | Re and |
| | assess- e cost | 1922 install- ment | Total assess- able cost | 1922 install- ment | Sewers | and water connections | Water pipe | |
|---|---|---|---|---|---|---|---|---|
| 27.13 | $ 337.86 | | | | | | | |
| | | | *$12,337.18 | $ 2,056.37 | | | | |
| 74.78 | 1,979.17 | | 40,092.89 | 6,683.31 | | | | |
| | | | 15,827.47 | 2,637.94 | | | | |
| | | | 46,453.59 | 7,742.83 | | | | |
| | | | 14,325.83 | 2,391.54 | | | | |
| 72.11 | 395.35 | | 21,294.00 | 3,549.18 | | | | |
| 98.06 | 3,882.98 | | 9,111.93 | 1,518.87 | | | | |
| 24.25 | 520.66 | | 4,743.76 | 790.69 | | | | |
| | | | 11,873.86 | 1,979.14 | | | | |
| | | | 17,953.85 | 4,439.33 | | 212.40 | 234.88 | |
| 48.05 | 2,275.08 | | 67,963.39 | 11,327.84 | 236.04 | | | |
| | | | 10,845.94 | 1,807.92 | | | | |
| 99.87 | 900.02 | | 17,067.78 | 2,844.63 | | 584.50 | | |
| | | | 1,595.79 | 265.97 | | | | |
| | | | 16,653.89 | 2,775.85 | 575.00 | | | |
| 87.98 | 797.98 | | 100,650.24 | 16,934.46 | | 9,108.90 | | |
| 68.02 | 611.43 | | 22,938.50 | 3,823.15 | | 460.50 | | |
| | | | 22,935.19 | 3,823.04 | | | | |
| 45.02 | 640.87 | | 138,438.88 | 23,076.65 | 29,359.05 | 35,032.70 | 34,335.28 | |
| 87.06 | 1,514.63 | | 105,806.86 | 17,635.14 | 2,671.07 | 8,392.10 | 3,976.61 | |
| 90.47 | 948.47 | | 159,366.61 | 26,739.53 | 2,752.80 | 7,932.80 | 7,212.02 | |
| 24.12 | 520.75 | | 11,498.16 | 1,916.54 | | | | |
| | | | 30,680.50 | 5,935.99 | 615.00 | 3,497.70 | | |
| 68.12 | 661.38 | | 47,076.99 | 7,848.85 | 178.32 | 6,718.00 | | |
| | $ 15,986.63 | | | $160,544.76 | $36,387.28 | $71,939.60 | $45,758.79 | |
| 15.04 | | | *$947,533.08 | | | | | |

x Total assessments for planting, pruning, spraying and removing trees

Street improvement installments prior to 1922................................$533,13
Street improvement installments (resurfacing) prior to 1922.......... 30,45

Total cost prior to 1922..................................................$563,58
Total 1922 .............................................................. 635,26

Grand total ....................................................................$1,198,85

totals for all work done, part of which is to be paid for by the property
e future. Hence they are not included in the totals.

| Removing earth from sidewalks | Cutting noxious weeds | Removing snow from sidewalks | Opening streets and alleys | Vacating streets and alleys | Miscellaneous | Grand total |
|---|---|---|---|---|---|---|
| --------- | $ 89.50 | $ 163.25 | --------- | --------- | $ 11.76 | $ 5,518.43 |
| --------- | 10.50 | 30.50 | $22,986.49 | --------- | 3.00 | 3,485.10 |
| --------- | 38.00 | 135.00 | 64,863.28 | --------- | --------- | 98,589.80 |
| --------- | 52.55 | 51.50 | --------- | --------- | --------- | 3,752.76 |
| --------- | 38.15 | 114.95 | --------- | --------- | 215.43 | 14,604.34 |
| 18.00 | 14.00 | 22.00 | --------- | --------- | +89.22 | 8,342.30 |
| --------- | 17.30 | 41.65 | --------- | --------- | 22.00 | 11,065.14 |
| --------- | --------- | 22.35 | --------- | --------- | 24.45 | 8,685.12 |
| --------- | 33.50 | 50.85 | --------- | --------- | --------- | 7,117.75 |
| --------- | 29.00 | 64.00 | --------- | --------- | 3,184.86 | 12,272.12 |
| --------- | 100.70 | 88.55 | 964.91 | --------- | 820.16 | 14,749.17 |
| --------- | 89.00 | 88.60 | --------- | --------- | 67.20 | 18,655.16 |
| --------- | 25.00 | 133.40 | --------- | --------- | 2.50 | 5,301.65 |
| 464.25 | 571.54 | 222.49 | --------- | --------- | 1,123.12 | 10,181.92 |
| --------- | 197.25 | 89.50 | --------- | --------- | 181.88 | 3,638.25 |
| --------- | 251.40 | 82.00 | --------- | --------- | 3,936.14 | 11,893.90 |
| 186.50 | 839.63 | 135.60 | --------- | --------- | 77.10 | 36,317.45 |
| 20.00 | 1,569.68 | 841.02 | --------- | --------- | 1,637.18 | 18,849.00 |
| 28.00 | 412.95 | 163.20 | --------- | --------- | 1,582.49 | 13,450.18 |
| --------- | 350.15 | 135.10 | 7,225.14 | $ 655.13 | 1,252.48 | 142,152.00 |
| 38.50 | 1,146.31 | 260.51 | 1,883.93 | --------- | 143.67 | 46,921.53 |
| --------- | 343.60 | 176.16 | 9,128.87 | --------- | 209.50 | 62,966.50 |
| 181.40 | 319.55 | 301.69 | 1,680.00 | --------- | --------- | 13,728.35 |
| --------- | 253.10 | 109.53 | 3,329.76 | --------- | 60.27 | 16,193.53 |
| 56.50 | 806.50 | 445.33 | --------- | --------- | 3.65 | 22,760.38 |
| --------- | --------- | --------- | --------- | --------- | 24,070.04 | 24,070.04 |
| $ 993.15 | $ 7,598.86 | $ 3,968.73 | $112,062.38 | $ 655.13 | $38,718.10 | $635,261.87 |

| | | | |
|---|---|---:|---:|
| ...d valuation is what per cent of true cash value | ------ | ------ | |
| ...' tax levy for library purposes | ------ | .0003 | .( |
| ...es in city and county, total number of | 125 | 240 | |
| ...te collections in city and county, total | ------ | 812 | |
| ...pen during year, number of (central library) | 303 | 363 | |
| ...open each week for lending (central library) | 72 | 78½ | |
| ...open each week for reading (central library) | 75 | 78½ | |
| **...tock** | | | |
| ...s at beginning of year, number of | 237,736 | 410,148 | 45 |
| ...s added during year by purchase, number of | 17,921 | 56,704 | 5 |
| ...s added during year by gift and exchange, number of | 1,923 | 1,871 | |
| ...s not otherwise counted, number of | 926 | ------ | |
| ...s lost or withdrawn during year, number of | 1,812 | 11,973 | 1 |
| ...s at end of year, number of | 256,694 | 456,750 | 49 |
| ...lets at beginning of year, number of | 18,284 | 23,862 | 2 |
| ...lets added during year, number of | 941 | 1,099 | |
| ...lets withdrawn during year, number of | ------ | 76 | |
| ...lets at end of year, total number of | 19,225 | 24,885 | 2 |
| ...s added at end of year, number of (estimated) | ------ | 2,000 | |
| ...s at end of year, total number of (estimated) | ------ | 9,000 | 1 |
| ...apers, periodicals, proceedings and transactions of learned so-ties currently received, number of | ------ | 605 | |
| ...s of fiction lent for home use, number of | 821,620 | 1,395,848 | 1,51 |
| ...s lent for home use, total number of | 1,149,646 | 2,199,359 | 2,47 |
| ...t fiction lent of total volumes lent | 71% | 63% | |
| ...tion per capita (city and county for 1921 and 1922) | 2.87 | 4. | |
| ...s lent for home use, number of | ------ | 7,654 | |
| **...ration** | | | |
| ...ers registered during year, number of | 15,361 | 39,093 | 3 |
| ...red borrowers, total number of | 58,394 | 96,483 | 10 |
| ...ation period, years | 4 | 3 | |
| ...nt registered borrowers of population (including county) served | 15% | 18 | |
| ...library service, full time | ------ | ------ | |
| ...library service, part time | ------ | ------ | |
| ...ervice, full time | ------ | ------ | |
| ...ervice, part time | ------ | ------ | |
| ...tal library service | ------ | 116 | |
| ...service, full time | ------ | ------ | |
| ...service, part time | ------ | ------ | |
| ...tal janitor service | ------ | 20 | |
| ...y service | ------ | 11 | |
| ...and total of staff | 80 | 147 | |

## BOOK DISTRIBUTING AGENCIES AND COLLECTIONS, 1922

...es in city and county, total number of

...te collections in city and county, total number of

| | Agencies | Sepa collec |
|---|---|---|
| ...tral library | 1 | 1 |
| ...nicipal reference library | 1 | 1 |
| ...nches | 11 | 11 |
| (3 occupy separate buildings) | | |
| ...-branches | 3 | 3 |
| ...h school branches | 5 | 5 |
| ...tions | 72 | 72 |
| ...er agencies: | | |
| City parochial and graded school buildings (includes 934 schoolroom collections) | 88 | 934 |
| High schools, colleges, academies, etc. (includes 30 separate collections) | 5 | 30 |

# PERSONNEL

JMBER AND CLASSIFICATION OF CITY EMPLOYES BY METHOD OF SELECTION
PAY-ROLL CHECK BY COMPTROLLER'S DEPARTMENT, JANUARY, 1923

| s under common council control | Number of Employes | Elective | Appointive | Appointive Under City Service Commission | Civil Service Fire and Police Commission | Teachi Staff |
|---|---|---|---|---|---|---|
| xaminers of engineers.................... | 3 | -- | 1 | 2 | ---- | ---- |
| re and police commissioners.......... | 2 | --- | --- | ---- | 2 | ---- |
| building and elevator inspection..... | 44 | -- | 1 | 43 | ---- | ---- |
| smoke suppression...................... | 4 | -- | 1 | 3 | ---- | ---- |
| rd of purchases......................... | 15 | -- | 4 | 11 | ---- | ---- |
| ey ........................................ | 12 | 1 | 6 | 4 | 1 | ---- |
| .............................................. | 8 | -- | 2 | 6 | ---- | ---- |
| rer ........................................ | 136 | 1 | 135* | ---- | ---- | ---- |
| ncil ....................................... | 27 | 25 | --- | 2 | ---- | ---- |
| roller .................................... | 24 | 1 | 1 | 22 | ---- | ---- |
| .............................................. | 15 | 3 | 12 | ---- | ---- | ---- |
| ment ...................................... | 685 | -- | 1 | ---- | 684 | ---- |
| lice alarm system...................... | 20 | -- | --- | ---- | 20 | ---- |
| artment ................................... | 255 | -- | 2 | 253 | ---- | ---- |
| mergency hospital...................... | 35 | -- | --- | 35 | ---- | ---- |
| he peace.................................. | 1 | 1 | --- | ---- | ---- | ---- |
| .............................................. | 3 | 1 | 2 | ---- | ---- | ---- |
| rtment .................................... | 743 | -- | 1 | ---- | 742 | ---- |
| commission.............................. | 18 | -- | 1 | 17 | ---- | ---- |
| s department: | | | | | | |
| office .................................... | 15 | -- | 2 | 13 | ---- | ---- |
| of engineers............................. | 35 | -- | 1 | 32 | ---- | ---- |
| of power plants......................... | 99 | -- | --- | 99 | ---- | ---- |
| of plumbing inspection................ | 9 | -- | --- | 9 | ---- | ---- |
| of sewers................................. | 76 | -- | 3** | 73 | ---- | ---- |
| of bridges and buildings.............. | 273 | -- | --- | 273 | ---- | ---- |
| of street construction and repairs.... | 41 | -- | --- | 41 | ---- | ---- |
| of street sanitation.................... | 1,174 | -- | 352*** | 822 | ---- | ---- |
| of electrical service.................... | 52 | -- | --- | 52 | ---- | ---- |
| of rivers and harbors.................. | 1 | -- | --- | 1 | ---- | ---- |
| eights and measures.................... | 9 | -- | --- | 9 | ---- | ---- |
| ment ...................................... | 32 | -- | 1 | 31 | ---- | ---- |
| otal ....................................... | 3,864 | 33 | 530 | 1,853 | 1,448 | ---- |
| 124 tax collection clerks. | | | | | | |
| 3 teams. | | | | | | |
| 352 teams. | | | | | | |
| ies: | | | | | | |
| epartment ............................... | 254 | -- | 3* | 251 | ---- | ---- |
| teams. | | | | | | |
| boards and commissions: | | | | | | |
| f election commissioners............. | 6 | -- | 3 | 3 | ---- | ---- |
| f harbor commissioners.............. | 8 | -- | --- | 8 | ---- | ---- |
| industrial education.................. | 328 | -- | 1 | 2 | ---- | 325* |
| vice commission....................... | 14 | -- | 5 | 9 | ---- | ---- |
| rd ......................................... | 258 | -- | 2** | 256 | ---- | ---- |
| brary .................................... | 153 | -- | --- | 153 | ---- | ---- |
| useum ................................... | 77 | -- | --- | 77 | ---- | ---- |
| ard ....................................... | 2,967 | 15 | 12 | 239 | ---- | 2,701** |
| e commission ........................... | 135 | -- | 2 | 133 | ---- | ---- |

189 evening teachers.

| | | |
|---|---:|---:|
| ation | | |
| ard of school directors | 5,339,675.72 | 4,560,901.91 |
| ard of industrial education | 469,895.99 | 283,438.42 |
| blic museum | 125,538.15 | 80,139.94 |
| storical museum | 81,151.51 | 47,140.57 |
| blic library | 249,752.29 | 130,734.38 |
| Totals for education | 6,266,013.66 | 5,102,355.22 |
| ic recreation | | |
| rk board | 492,392.64 | 305,520.66 |
| l government | | |
| ty service commission | 25,634.98 | 22,492.92 |
| Total not including expenditures for improvements | 6,784,041.28 | 5,430,368.80 |
| direct control of common council | | |
| ral government: | | |
| Executive, legislative and judicial group | | |
| ayor | 12,727.83 | 10,789.92 |
| mmon council | 65,399.23 | 50,360.00 |
| ty clerk | 16,125.76 | 14,520.03 |
| ty attorney | 53,607.75 | 35,738.18 |
| urts | 50,242.72 | 35,012.49 |
| ection commission | 59,503.87 | 39,120.04 |
| Total | 257,607.16 | 185,540.66 |
| ral government: | | |
| Finance group | | |
| mptroller | 53,533.65 | 39,910.01 |
| reasurer | 98,609.74 | 81,756.87 |
| ix department | 71,210.86 | 68,199.96 |
| blic debt commission | 10,471.32 | 1,620.00 |
| ntral board of purchases | 30,643.76 | 25,929.41 |
| Total | 264,469.33 | 217,416.25 |
| tion of life and property | | |
| pard of fire and police commissioners | 1,572.87 | 1,539.00 |
| re department | 1,435,093.99 | 1,205,259.96 |
| lice department | 1,314,923.76 | 1,249,505.21 |
| re and police alarm system | 105,525.79 | 58,297.30 |
| aler of weights and measures | 24,638.56 | 17,460.00 |
| reau of building and elevator inspection | 77,916.26 | 71,767.37 |
| pard of examiners of engineers | 7,125.51 | 6,480.00 |
| Total | 2,966,796.74 | 2,610,308.84 |
| health and sanitation | | |
| ealth department | 420,163.95 | 342,155.28 |
| hnson emergecy hospital | 48,370.45 | 33,606.02 |
| reau of smoke suppression | 7,521.90 | 7,434.19 |
| reau of street sanitation | 1,346,535.91 | 1,254,051.93 |
| reau of plumbing inspection | 27,092.94 | 25,828.00 |
| reau of sewers | 92,999.39 | 74,762.53 |
| Total | 1,942,684.54 | 1,737,837.95 |
| tion of economic welfare | | |
| artment of public works | | |
| eneral administration | 33,698.55 | 27,571.75 |
| reau of bridges and buildings | 696,196.75 | 481,008.82 |
| reau of engineers | 67,487.79 | 61,766.68 |
| reau of street construction and repairs | 168,831.95 | 159,208.51 |
| reau of rivers and harbors | 40,227.68 | 3,319.00 |
| reau of power plants | 241,374.76 | 189,749.33 |
| rd of public land commissioners | 30,031.64 | 22,309.25 |
| Total | 1,277,849.12 | 954,933.34 |

PUBLIC UTILITIES

## MARRIAGES
### NATIVITY OF THE CONTRACTING PARTIES

| | Groom | Bride | Both |
|---|---|---|---|
| | 248 | 399 | 722 |
| | 456 | 675 | 1454 |
| s | 486 | 326 | 176 |
| | 132 | 111 | 49 |
| | 98 | 44 | 102 |
| | 79 | 71 | 113 |
| | 56 | 25 | 52 |
| | 30 | 2 | 23 |
| | 25 | 22 | 69 |
| | 22 | 25 | 4 |
| | 9 | -- | 29 |
| | 12 | 6 | 3 |
| | 5 | 2 | 1 |
| | 6 | 4 | 2 |
| | 1 | 1 | 3 |
| | 23 | 9 | 1 |
| | 6 | 3 | 2 |
| | 4 | 3 | 1 |
| | 47 | 19 | 46 |
| | 1 | 1 | 0 |

| AGE | Groom | Brid |
|---|---|---|
| Under age | 163 | 12 |
| 21 to 25 | 1441 | 265 |
| 26 to 35 | 2254 | 136 |
| 36 to 45 | 473 | 29 |
| 46 to 55 | 175 | 11 |
| 56 to 65 | 80 | 4 |
| 66 to 75 | 13 | |

### SOCIAL CONDITION

| | Groom | Brid |
|---|---|---|
| Oldest (age) | 73 | 6 |
| Youngest (age) | 18 | 1 |
| Widowed (number) | 394 | 32 |
| Divorced (number) | 231 | 26 |
| Colored (number) | 21 | 2 |

### RESIDENCE

| | Groom | Brid |
|---|---|---|
| Milwaukee | 3836 | 415 |
| Outside city | 560 | 37 |
| Outside state | 203 | 7 |

### CEREMONY PERFORMED

| | |
|---|---|
| By ministers | 387 |
| By judges | 28 |
| By justices | 41 |

## BIRTH STATISTICS

### GENERAL

| | |
|---|---|
| | 10,563 |
| s | 10,218 |
| | 345 |
| ousand | 22.2 |
| | 5,446 |
| | 5,117 |
| | 10,502 |
| | 61 |
| ins | 8,914 |
| es | 1,433 |
| | 216 |
| spitals | 2,709 |
| de city | 63 |
| births | 230 |
| legitimate births | 90 |
| | 111 |

### BY WARDS

| | | | |
|---|---|---|---|
| First | 468 | Fifteenth | 22 |
| Second | 339 | Sixteenth | 23 |
| Third | 367 | Seventeenth | 46 |
| Fourth | 289 | Eighteenth | 29 |
| Fifth | 339 | Nineteenth | 36 |
| Sixth | 411 | Twentieth | 57 |
| Seventh | 363 | Twenty-first | 45 |
| Eighth | 471 | Twenty-second | 46 |
| Ninth | 407 | Twenty-third | 41 |
| Tenth | 313 | Twenty-fourth | 47 |
| Eleventh | 456 | Twenty-fifth | 35 |
| Twelfth | 430 | Transient | 50 |
| Thirteenth | 457 | Unknown | |
| Fourteenth | 629 | | |

### NATIVITY OF PARENT

| | Father | Mother | Both Parent |
|---|---|---|---|
| Milwaukee | 335 | 610 | 90 |
| Wisconsin | 836 | 1438 | 331 |
| United States | 878 | 847 | 73 |
| Germany | 387 | 246 | 24 |
| Poland | 361 | 110 | 62 |
| Austria | 130 | 82 | 22 |
| Russia | 90 | 47 | 21 |
| Italy | 61 | 6 | 32 |
| Hungary | 40 | 27 | 15 |
| England | 60 | 44 | 1 |
| Greece | 28 | -- | 7 |
| Norway | 18 | 10 | |

### AGE OF MOTHER

| Births | Age | Births |
|---|---|---|
| 2 | 33 | 380 |
| 9 | 34 | 345 |
| 36 | 35 | 285 |
| 70 | 36 | 227 |
| 167 | 37 | 250 |
| 378 | 38 | 234 |
| 439 | 39 | 160 |
| 546 | 40 | 154 |
| 612 | 41 | 74 |
| 659 | 42 | 76 |

| | Number | of total | ing births per t |
|---|---|---|---|
| deaths of all ages | 4676 | 100 | -- |
| deaths under thirty days of age | 439 | 9 | 43 |
| deaths from thirty days to one year | 383 | 8 | 36 |
| deaths from one year to five years | 240 | 5 | -- |
| deaths—still born | 345 | 7 | -- |

## INFANT MORTALITY, UNDER FIVE YEARS, 1910-1922

| Year | Total deaths | Under 30 days | 30 days to 1 year | 1 to 5 years | Total Under 5 years | Per cent under 1 to total | Per cent under 5 to total | Under 30 days to 1,000 births | Under 1 year to 1,000 births |
|---|---|---|---|---|---|---|---|---|---|
| | 5199 | 501 | 868 | 474 | 1843 | 26 | 35 | 53 | 145 |
| | 4717 | 478 | 739 | 343 | 1560 | 26 | 33 | 46 | 116 |
| | 5196 | 489 | 891 | 454 | 1834 | 26 | 35 | 47 | 133 |
| | 5159 | 594 | 631 | 442 | 1667 | 24 | 33 | 55 | 113 |
| | 4920 | 550 | 569 | 427 | 1546 | 23 | 31 | 48 | 97 |
| | 4868 | 491 | 580 | 337 | 1408 | 22 | 29 | 41 | 99 |
| | 5545 | 564 | 683 | 515 | 1762 | 22 | 31 | 50 | 113 |
| | 5453 | 515 | 589 | 405 | 1509 | 20 | 28 | 46 | 99 |
| | 6598 | 557 | 666 | 652 | 1875 | 18 | 28 | 49 | 108 |
| | 5012 | 501 | 525 | 358 | 1384 | 21 | 28 | 47 | 98 |
| | 5395 | 505 | 467 | 399 | 1371 | 18 | 25 | 45 | 89 |
| | 4568 | 521 | 351 | 319 | 1291 | 19 | 28 | 46 | 81 |
| | 4676 | 439 | 383 | 240 | 1062 | 17 | 22 | 43 | 79 |

## AVERAGE AGE AT DEATH, 1879-1922

| Year | All ages | Over five years | Year | All Ages | Over fiv |
|---|---|---|---|---|---|
| 1879 | 18.1 | 44.3 | 1901 | 33.3 | 49. |
| 1880 | 18.1 | 39.5 | 1902 | 31.6 | 48. |
| 1881 | 17. | 35.4 | 1903 | 33. | 48. |
| 1882 | 18.8 | 42.2 | 1904 | 32.2 | 48. |
| 1883 | 20. | 42. | 1905 | 27.1 | 48. |
| 1884 | 18.2 | 43.8 | 1906 | 32. | 49. |
| 1885 | 20.4 | 43.7 | 1907 | 33.6 | 49. |
| 1886 | 20. | 43. | 1908 | 32.1 | 49. |
| 1887 | 19.9 | 46.2 | 1909 | 30.8 | 47. |
| 1888 | 20.6 | 43.4 | 1910 | 31.8 | 48. |
| 1889 | 21. | 44.2 | 1911 | 34.5 | 49. |
| 1890 | 21.9 | 43. | 1912 | 33. | 49. |
| 1891 | 20.6 | 42.3 | 1913 | 34.7 | 51. |
| 1892 | 22.2 | 42.6 | 1914 | 34.4 | 50. |
| 1893 | 22.2 | 44.2 | 1915 | 37.8 | 53. |
| 1894 | 22.3 | 43.9 | 1916 | 36.6 | 52. |
| 1895 | 24.7 | 45.7 | 1917 | 37.8 | 51. |
| 1896 | 25.5 | 45.8 | 1918 | 33.6 | 47. |
| 1897 | 27.9 | 46.8 | 1919 | 38.5 | 51. |
| 1898 | 29 | 49.6 | 1920 | 38.7 | 51. |

| | 1914 | | 1915 | | 1916 | | 1917 | | 1918 | | 1919 | | 1920 | | 1921 | | 192– |
|---|---|---|---|---|---|---|---|---|---|---|---|---|---|---|---|---|---|
| | 4920 | | 4868 | | 5545 | | 5453 | | 6598 | | 5012 | | 5395 | | 4568 | | 4… |
| 00.. | 12.15 | | 11.73 | | 12.89 | | 12.40 | | 14.82 | | 11.00 | | 11.61 | | 9.61 | | 9… |
| | Cases | Deaths | Cases | Deaths | Cases | Deaths | Cases | Deaths | Cases | Deaths | Cases | Deaths | Cases | Deaths | Cases | Deaths | Cases |
| | 123 | 33 | 95 | 19 | 511 | 64 | 89 | 26 | 103 | 28 | 47 | 16 | 37 | 10 | 36 | 9 | 34 |
| | 1157 | --- | 221 | --- | 23 | --- | 116 | --- | 206 | 1 | 332 | --- | 568 | --- | 517 | --- | 112 |
| | 1340 | 19 | 1400 | 10 | 6209 | 101 | 1518 | 10 | 6394 | 54 | 410 | 1 | 5827 | 19 | 305 | 1 | 5681 |
| | 1138 | 80 | 471 | 24 | 1584 | 41 | 3219 | 69 | 1327 | 51 | 1118 | 22 | 1287 | 29 | 1322 | 54 | 1151 |
| h.... | 136 | 6 | 1452 | 40 | 1212 | 30 | 1400 | 48 | 1636 | 46 | 1028 | 22 | 1913 | 53 | 869 | 8 | 3256 |
| | 1133 | 134 | 693 | 96 | 716 | 73 | 787 | 99 | 430 | 51 | 1017 | 96 | 1576 | 119 | 1404 | 84 | 816 |
| | --- | --- | --- | 15 | --- | 37 | --- | 81 | 18339 | 403 | 1267 | 82 | 2601 | 108 | 2 | 7 | 35 |
| lm. | 957 | 356 | 979 | 353 | 1017 | 329 | 962 | 370 | 1115 | 399 | 904 | 315 | 903 | 322 | 835 | 246 | 689 |
| | --- | 270 | --- | 336 | --- | 374 | --- | 331 | --- | 352 | --- | 361 | --- | 382 | --- | 388 | --- |
| | --- | 56 | --- | 59 | --- | 69 | --- | 66 | --- | 92 | 67 | 63 | 72 | 72 | 35 | 43 | 44 |
| Org. | --- | 258 | --- | 243 | --- | 282 | --- | 262 | --- | 237 | --- | 292 | --- | 306 | --- | 313 | --- |
| | --- | 337 | --- | 364 | --- | 418 | --- | 429 | --- | 415 | --- | 431 | --- | 481 | --- | 484 | --- |
| | --- | 121 | --- | 141 | --- | 143 | --- | 129 | --- | 128 | --- | 105 | --- | 76 | --- | 88 | --- |
| on. | --- | 511 | --- | 637 | --- | 726 | --- | 792 | --- | 1636 | --- | 716 | 528 | 930 | 263 | 404 | 325 |
| | --- | --- | --- | 3 | 16 | 2 | 10 | 3 | 94 | 24 | 90 | 13 | 8 | 1 | 32 | 6 | 8 |
| r 2 | --- | 239 | --- | 194 | --- | 263 | --- | 238 | --- | 234 | --- | 209 | --- | 187 | --- | 140 | --- |
| | --- | 258 | --- | 282 | --- | 301 | --- | 329 | --- | 293 | --- | 301 | --- | 260 | --- | 255 | --- |
| | --- | 380 | --- | 309 | --- | 393 | --- | 303 | --- | 237 | --- | 271 | --- | 266 | --- | 275 | --- |
| | --- | 114 | --- | 127 | --- | 109 | --- | 97 | --- | 72 | --- | 85 | --- | 115 | --- | 101 | --- |
| | --- | 340 | --- | 285 | --- | 375 | --- | 407 | --- | 343 | --- | 305 | --- | 280 | --- | 316 | --- |
| | --- | 88 | --- | 70 | --- | 69 | --- | 83 | --- | 69 | --- | 65 | --- | 53 | --- | 84 | --- |
| | --- | 22 | --- | 14 | --- | 8 | --- | 28 | --- | 19 | --- | 11 | --- | 14 | --- | 17 | --- |
| | --- | --- | --- | --- | --- | --- | --- | --- | --- | --- | --- | --- | --- | --- | --- | --- | 79 |
| | --- | --- | --- | --- | --- | --- | --- | --- | --- | --- | --- | --- | --- | --- | --- | --- | 86 |
| | --- | --- | --- | --- | --- | --- | --- | --- | --- | --- | --- | --- | --- | --- | --- | --- | 1725 |
| | --- | --- | --- | --- | --- | --- | --- | --- | --- | --- | --- | --- | --- | --- | --- | --- | 1600 |

## CONTAGIOUS DISEASES BY WARDS

| | Typhoid Fever | | Small-pox | | Measles | | Scarlet Fever | | Whooping Cough | | Diphtheria | | Tubc. Pulm. | |
|---|---|---|---|---|---|---|---|---|---|---|---|---|---|---|
| | Cases | Deaths | Cases | Deaths | Cases | Deaths | Cases | Deaths | Cases | Deaths | Cases | Deaths | Cases | Deaths |
| | 3 | 1 | 2 | --- | 173 | --- | 18 | --- | 108 | 1 | 47 | 2 | 23 | |
| | 1 | --- | 5 | --- | 179 | --- | 19 | --- | 91 | 2 | 38 | 1 | 29 | |
| | 5 | 1 | 1 | --- | 111 | --- | 59 | 5 | 35 | --- | 57 | 2 | 49 | |
| | 1 | 1 | 2 | --- | 48 | --- | 32 | 1 | 60 | --- | 17 | 2 | 32 | |
| | --- | --- | 5 | --- | 402 | 1 | 38 | --- | 180 | 1 | 17 | 2 | 38 | |
| | 4 | 2 | 7 | --- | 132 | --- | 40 | --- | 132 | --- | 25 | 1 | 31 | |
| | 3 | 1 | 8 | 1 | 170 | --- | 31 | --- | 133 | 1 | 42 | 2 | 13 | 1 |
| | --- | --- | --- | --- | 407 | 1 | 114 | 1 | 118 | --- | 38 | 1 | 30 | 1 |
| | 1 | 1 | 4 | --- | 235 | 1 | 81 | 1 | 144 | 2 | 44 | 2 | 23 | 1 |
| | 1 | --- | 1 | --- | 134 | --- | 45 | --- | 97 | 1 | 25 | 3 | 28 | |
| | --- | --- | 11 | 1 | 340 | 1 | 74 | --- | 113 | 1 | 51 | 7 | 26 | 1 |
| | 1 | --- | 4 | --- | 353 | --- | 39 | --- | 142 | 1 | 24 | 3 | 26 | |
| | --- | --- | --- | --- | 391 | --- | 35 | --- | 133 | --- | 39 | 4 | 30 | |
| | --- | --- | 2 | --- | 260 | 1 | 44 | --- | 170 | 2 | 37 | 5 | 26 | 1 |
| | 1 | --- | 1 | --- | 257 | --- | 26 | 2 | 98 | --- | 20 | --- | 7 | |
| | 1 | --- | 2 | --- | 330 | --- | 32 | 1 | 125 | --- | 18 | 1 | 26 | |
| | 1 | --- | 28 | --- | 311 | --- | 23 | --- | 133 | 1 | 19 | 1 | 21 | |

ing revenues (water only)........................................ $ 1,95
ing expenditures ............................................... $ 566,838.79
ing expenditures (parks)........................................ 14,315.68
iation ......................................................... 135,507.00    71

                                                                            $1,242

operating revenues............................................. 75,226.92
operating expenditures......................................... 54,654.49

                                                                               2

ial revenue ...................................................

income from operation.......................................... $ 1,26
ion from above—interest on bonded debt.........................

:ome from operation............................................ $ 1,25
revenues received—water pipe assessment (tax levy 1922) ....... 4
ater pipe assessment (old city boundaries)....................
ivate water pipe acquired by annexation.......................

1et income from all sources................................... $ 1,30

## DISPOSITION OF NET INCOME

er to general city fund........................................ 225,000.00
ered to unreserved city proprietary interest.................. $ 1,083,422.89
                                                                            $ 1,30
mount expended for new construction work and outlays during the year 1922   $ 1,30
roprietary interest December 31, 1922......................... 12,72
ost of water works, less depreciation......................... 12,10
l indebtedness, less sinking fund on hand.....................    15

## ESTIMATED COST OF SUPPLYING WATER TO CONSUMERS

f operation (including parks).................................. $  581,154.47
t on bonded debt..............................................    7,425.00

rdinary expenditures.......................................... $   58
g fund for bonded indebtedness................................ 15,000.00
iation ....................................................... 135,507.00
on true value of water works property......................... 272,447.68
st on net invested capital at four per cent................... 484,394.49

                                                                         $   90

                                                                         $ 1,49

## REVENUE

revenue for water only........................................ $ 1,95
ie per thousand gallons based on total pumpage................

## COST OF SUPPLYING WATER PER THOUSAND GALLONS

| | 1 | 2 | 3 | 4 | 5 | |
|---|---|---|---|---|---|---|
| | | gallons | gallons | and stores gallons | gallons | |
| red consumption | | 1,273,351,240 | 7,837,371,367 | 7,939,570,085 | 17,050,292,692 | 7 |
| l flat rate consumption | | 869,048,446 | 77,158,000 | 1,389,000 | 947,595,446 | 4 |
| free use | | | | | 209,845,230 | |
| istration of meters (estimated at three nt of water passed through meters) | | | | | 527,328,640 | |
| ted for" | | | | | 3,729,467,608 | 1 |
| | | 2,142,399,686 | 7,914,529,367 | 7,940,959,085 | 22,464,529,616 | 100 |

pumpage based on plunger displacement of pumps—23,646,873,280 gallons, less five per cent estima
f pumps—22,464,529,616 gallons delivered into distribution mains.

## DAILY CONSUMPTION FOR THE LAST FIVE YEARS

| Year | Gallons | Year | Gallons |
|---|---|---|---|
| 1918 | 62,598,948 | 1921 | 62,334,792 |
| 1919 | 61,891,603 | 1922 | 64,785,954 |
| 1920 | 66,900,560 | | |

## BACTERIOLOGICAL TESTS OF LAKE MICHIGAN WATER
(As reported by the water works laboratory.)

of Bacteria in One Cubic Centimeter of Water and Percentage of Reduction by Use of Chlorine

| | | Before Treatment with Chlorine | | | After Treatment with Chlorine | | | Per cent Reduct by Use of Chlor |
|---|---|---|---|---|---|---|---|---|
| | | Maximum | Minimum | Mean | Maximum | Minimum | Mean | |
| | 20°C | 48,000 | 4 | 3,114 | 20,300 | 0 | 473 | 86.51 |
| n | 20°C | 36,500 | 0 | 1,472 | 13,600 | 0 | 221 | 86.70 |
| | 37°C | 27,000 | 0 | 443 | 7,200 | 0 | 53 | 85.27 |

n and agar at 20°C incubated forty-eight hours, agar at 37°C incubated twenty-four hours.

## PERCENTAGE OF GAS FORMERS PRESENT.
(Presumptive test.)

| e of sample. | | Before treatment. | After treatmen |
|---|---|---|---|
| ubic centimeters | | 76.8 | 30.0 |
| ubic centimeter | | 41.7 | 7.8 |
| ubic centimeter | | 12.3 | 1.3 |
| ubic centimeter | | 0.0 | 0.0 |

## BACILLUS COLI INDEX.
(Confirmed tests.)

| | Before treatment | | | After treatment | | |
|---|---|---|---|---|---|---|
| | maximum | minimum | mean | maximum | minimum | mean |
| centimeter | 10 | 0 | 2.88 | 10 | 0 | .363 |
| ubic centimeters | | | 288 | | | 36 |

United States public health service has fixed the standard of purity for drinking water supplied
common carriers at two bacilli coli per one hundred cubic centimeters of water.

## AGE CHEMICAL ANALYSIS OF RAW LAKE MICHIGAN WATER IN PARTS PER MILLION
(Based on weekly analysis.)

| as | | |
|---|---|---|
| e ammonia (NH3) | | . |
| umenoid ammonia (NH3) | | . |
| rites | | . |
| rates | | . |
| onsumed | | 3. |

(In form recommended by the New England Water Works Association.)

## GENERAL STATISTICS.

pulation by census of 1920—457,174.  Present population estimated at 485,000.
te of original construction—1872-1874.
 whom owned—city of Milwaukee.
de of supply (whether gravity or pumping)—pumping.

## PUMPING STATISTICS.

ilders of pumping machinery—Edward P. Allis Co., Allis-Chalmers Mfg. Co., Wisconsin Engi
) Total pumping capacity:
 North Point station—nominal 126,000,000 gallons in 24 hours.
                     actual   150,000,000 gallons in 24 hours.
 High Service station—nominal 25,000,000 gallons in 24 hours.

scription of fuel used:
) Kind bituminous.
) Brand of coal—Pocahontas screenings and Eastern screenings.
) Price of coal per ton of 2000 lbs., delivered by truck to pumping stations.
 North Point station:
   Pocahontas screenings _____ $5.50 t
   Eastern screenings _____  5.65 t
 High Service station:
   Eastern screenings _____  5.60 t
   Pocahontas screenings _____  5.60 t
) Percentage of ash of coal consumed at North Point pumping station—12.92.
) Percentage of ash of coal consumed at High Service pumping station—13.21.
) Wood, price per cord—none used.

al consumed:
) North Point pumping station (for all purposes)_____ 38,516,
) North Point pumping station (while pumping) _____ 37,750,
) High Service pumping station (for all purposes)_____  1,995,
) High Service pumping station (while pumping) _____  1,622,

unds of wood consumed÷3=equivalent amount of coal—none.
) Amount of other fuel used—none.

tal equivalent coal consumed for the year (4) lbs.—none.

tal pumpage for the year:
) North Point pumping station (where all direct pumpage from the lake is done) 23,646,873,28
) High Service pumping station (where the water is re-pumped from the reservoir into the hig
     ice district)—1,461,096,900 gallons.

erage static head against which pumps work (North Point pumping station low service)—150 f

erage dynamic head against which pumps work:
) North Point pumping station, low service 156.665; high service 284.015.  Average of high a
     service—218.440 feet.
) High service pumping station 122.577 feet+suction head 8.122 feet+128.30 feet elevation of
     =258.999 ft. above datum.

mber of gallons pumped per pound of equivalent coal (5)—none.

ty $\left\{ \dfrac{\text{Gals. pumped (6.A) x 8.34 (lbs.) x 100 x dynamic head (8.A.)}}{\text{Total fuel consumed while pumping at North Point pumping station (3B).}} \right.$ =114,132,015 lb

## STATISTICS OF CONSUMPTION OF WATER.

ated total population at date (city only) _____ 485,0
ated population on lines of pipe (city only) _____ 485,0
ated population supplied (includes suburbs) _____ 520,0
consumption for the year_____ 23,646,873,280 ga
d through meters_____ 17,050,292,692 ga
ntage of consumption metered_____ 72.
age daily consumption_____ 64,785,954 ga
ns per day to each inhabitant (1) after deducting water furnished outside of city___ 115.68 ga
ns per day to each inhabitant, including population supplied outside of city (3) _____ 124.5  ga
ns per day to each tap_____ 909.  ga
This is figured on taps in actual use, of which number 70,298 are metered, 170 elevator
ndicators and 741 unmetered. The latter consists of 480 automatic fire sprinkler connec-
ions with street mains, public drinking troughs, bubblers, etc.)
of supplying water per million gallons, figured on total operating and maintenance expenditures, i
g depreciation ($716,661.47)—$30.30.
of supplying water per million gallons, figured on total operating and maintenance expenditures, i
g depreciation, plus interest on bonds—$30.62.

ion for slippage, estimated at 5%.


## STATISTICS RELATING TO DISTRIBUTION SYSTEM MAINS.

of pipe—cast iron.
from 4 to 54 inch.
ded 79,328 lineal feet; annexed 1,722 lineal feet—15.024 miles.
ntinued lineal feet—5470—.104 miles.
now in use—575 miles.
of repairs per mile, including valves and boxes—$14.15.
ber of leaks per mile—.19.
th of pipe less than 4 inches in diameter—None.
ber of hydrants added during the year—114; cut out 10.
ber of hydrants now in use—3987.
ber of stop gates added during the year—281; annexed, 1; cut out, 3.
ber of stop gates now in use—5037.
ber of stop gates smaller than 4 inch—1.
ddition to the above gates, there are 2536 gates from 2 to 8 inches, controlling branch connections
ber of blow offs—84.
e of pressure on mains—20 to 90 pounds.
8, 19, 20, 23, 24. All services put in by consumer.
ber of services (taps and branches) added during the year—2,264.
ber of services connected to mains—90,999 taps and 2536 branches, a total of 93,535.
ber of new meters added during the year—2210.
ber of meters now in use—70,298, after deducting 350 meters permanently off.
ntage of services metered—98.72.
ntage of receipts from metered water—87.92.
ber of motors and elevators added—none—5 taken out.
ber now in use—170.

Lightning Source UK Ltd.
Milton Keynes UK
UKHW05f0705100918
328632UK00007B/649/P